I0804743

NO FLESH SHALL GLORY

What a privilege to sit under the teaching of this civil rights icon through the pages of *No Flesh Shall Glory*. With the heart of a pastor and the careful exegesis of a scholar, Pastor Oliver pushes against historic presuppositions for interpreting race and offers sound scriptural argument, exposing the heart of God and inviting the reader to see with new eyes. This will be the resource on race and culture you will return to over and over again. I can't recommend this book enough!

—**Vanessa K. Hawkins**, Director of Women's Ministry, First Presbyterian Church, Augusta, Georgia; Diversity Advisor, PCA Women's Ministry

Reflecting on the difference between the changes in the law during the civil rights era and the rigidity of the church, Rev. C. Herbert Oliver bemoaned, "Christians seem to learn more slowly than the children of darkness, for the world seems to be leading the way in the battle against the dogmas of racism." For Rev. Oliver, remaining separate and segregated in the church is anti-Christian. In *No Flesh Shall Glory*, he calls us to embrace the truth that our God is a God of variety and to rejoice in the limitless display of God's creative genius in that variety. "If God loves variety, it is perverse for men to hate it," he writes. I am grateful to P&R Publishing for bringing this book and this man of God before a new generation. What he writes here is not just a blessing and benefit for a time gone by, but it is needful for us today. This work is part of the necessary antidote to our ongoing fractures and polarization within the body of Christ. He points us to the heart of God for humanity.

—**Irwyn L. Ince**, Director, GraceDC Institute for Cross-Cultural Mission; Author, *The Beautiful Community: Unity, Diversity, and the Church at Its Best*

C. Herbert Oliver's classic study is well entitled *No Flesh Shall Glory*. It is perhaps needed more now than when it first appeared in 1959. Oliver leads readers to Scripture and demonstrates that prevailing concepts of race and practices of segregation are deeply inconsistent with God's creation of all mankind in His image. *No Flesh Shall Glory* is a biblical antidote to contemporary critical race theories that foment racial tensions and diminish commitment to the Lordship of Christ and the reconciling power of His kingdom. I am grateful that Oliver's prophetic ministry speaks again in these troubled times.

—**Peter A. Lillback**, President, Westminster Theological Seminary

C. Herbert Oliver's book *No Flesh Shall Glory* is as riveting and relevant today as when it was first published in 1959. Writing with theological precision, Oliver delivers a passionate plea for Christians to embrace the biblical doctrines of race that align with both God's character and His plan for the church. Specifically, he connects the wisdom of God in creating diverse ethnicities to the power of God in unifying all peoples in one family. This good news is as timeless as it is timely!

—**Doug Logan Jr.**, President, Grimké Seminary; Associate Director, Acts 29 Global Network; Author, *On the Block: Developing a Biblical Picture for Missional Engagement*

When this biblically based, theologically informed, anti-racist book was first published, it was ahead of its time. Written by C. Herbert Oliver—a principled pastor who was educated at Wheaton College and Westminster Theological Seminary—*No Flesh Shall Glory* makes a clear biblical case for the beauty of kingdom diversity and the absolute unity of the human race created in the image of God. As an outspoken critic of police brutality in Bull Connor's Birmingham and an advocate for just public education in Brooklyn, New York, Oliver has lived by these principles ever since. Both the man and this book are anti-racist for the simple reason that racism is anti-Christian.

—**Philip Ryken**, President, Wheaton College

NO FLESH SHALL GLORY

HOW THE BIBLE DESTROYS THE FOUNDATIONS OF RACISM

C. HERBERT OLIVER

P&R
PUBLISHING
P.O. BOX 817 • PHILLIPSBURG • NEW JERSEY 08865-0817

No Flesh Shall Glory © 1959 by The Presbyterian and Reformed Publishing Company
New edition © 2021 by P&R Publishing

All rights reserved. No part of this book may be reproduced, stored in a retrieval system, or transmitted in any form or by any means—electronic, mechanical, photocopy, recording, or otherwise—except for brief quotations for the purpose of review or comment, without the prior permission of the publisher, P&R Publishing Company, P.O. Box 817, Phillipsburg, New Jersey 08865-0817.

Italics within Scripture quotations indicate emphasis added.

C. Herbert Oliver, "The Church and Social Change," was delivered in two lectures under the auspices of the Harry Worcester Lectureship at Westminster Theological Seminary on March 31, 1964, and April 1, 1964, and later printed in *Presbyterian Guardian* 33, no. 6 (1964): 87–94. It has been lightly edited for this volume. Used by permission.

Printed in the United States of America

Library of Congress Cataloging-in-Publication Data

Names: Oliver, C. Herbert, 1925- author.
Title: No flesh shall glory : how the Bible destroys the foundations of racism : also includes "the church and social change" / C. Herbert Oliver.
Description: New edition. | Phillipsburg : P&R Publishing, 2021. | Summary: "Clear, biblical, and unflinching, civil rights leader Rev. C. Herbert Oliver dismantles the dogmas of race superiority and the doctrine of racial solidarity. "In God's sight no flesh shall glory.""-- Provided by publisher.
Identifiers: LCCN 2020049204 | ISBN 9781629959016 (paperback)
Subjects: LCSH: Race. | Segregation--Religious aspects. | Sociology, Biblical.
Classification: LCC BT734 .O4 2021 | DDC 241/.675--dc23
LC record available at https://lccn.loc.gov/2020049204

To my wife and my father

1959

CONTENTS

EDITOR'S NOTE

You are holding a piece of history—a book written more than sixty years ago by a man who had a passion to see justice done in the world, and particularly in the United States of America. At that time, many white Christians promoted the separation of the races and tried to defend it as compatible with Christian ethics. Interracial marriage was viewed as a sin. For some, even the casual or friendly association of Black and white people was suspect. A grievous embrace of worldly racial ideology made this book necessary, and Rev. C. Herbert Oliver, with bold commitment to biblical truth, rose to meet that need. He did more than write. In 1959, the year this book was originally published, he moved from Maine back to his hometown of Birmingham, Alabama, to participate as an activist in the civil rights movement.

Is there need for this book today? We believe that there is. Rev. Oliver's reliance on the Word of God fills his writing with enduring wisdom as he speaks of the complex nature of humankind. He writes as one of God's champions of truth, graciously and firmly, and so we can learn from both his message and the way in which he conveys it.

The need for this book, however, goes deeper than this. When truths about human beings are exchanged for lies, the damage is profound. Worldly racial ideologies remain with us to this day, often in new forms. As the world and the church continue to grapple with racism and related issues, we would do well to listen to the insights of a man who took up the fight in decades past. We are grateful to Rev. Oliver for his bold commitment to this cause.

We are also grateful to Mr. Charles H. Craig, who in the 1950s helped to promote a message so controversial in its day. Mr. Craig had headed Presbyterian and Reformed Publishing Company for only two years when he published *No Flesh Shall Glory*. He had an interest in social causes—having formerly been involved with Big Brothers of New York City—and a desire to promote biblical understanding on a wide range of issues.

Rev. Oliver writes as a graduate of Wheaton College and Westminster Theological Seminary and as a pastor in the Orthodox Presbyterian Church—in a style both pastoral and academic. Thus, although *No Flesh Shall Glory* has some technical elements, it is broadly accessible. We have made very few changes to the text. His 1964 paper "The Church and Social Change" has immediate application for discussions today and is a good starting point for those getting acquainted with his work. We are delighted to be able to include it in this volume as well.

PREFACE

The subject of the present discourse has engaged my most serious study for thirteen years. At one time my notions about race differed little from the popular notions that surrounded me, even "interracial marriage" being considered a great sin. Without question I imbibed the prevailing sentiments about the "races." In 1943, however, a series of circumstances combined to confront me with the task of reevaluating my position with the purpose of arriving at a position that I could intelligently call my own. I had expected that a little investigation would suffice to give me the desired understanding. But the subject was broader than I had expected it to be; and after years of study and contemplation, I would be the last to say that I have delivered the last word on "race." My teachers have been books and human nature. There is a Higher Teacher, however, whose Word, the Bible, has been my most basic source of information and inspiration. That Word, which liveth and abideth forever, is a most sufficient guide in matters of faith and conduct, and the eternal truths of its pages are wonderfully applicable today to a problem that confronts not only this nation but also the world.

It is my most sincere prayer to the God and Father of our Lord Jesus Christ, of whom the whole family in heaven and earth is named, that He may use this book to correct, reprove and instruct in that righteousness that is unto eternal life and unto good human relations.

Various friends have given valuable criticisms of the manuscript for which I am grateful. Among them are Mr. Murray F. Thompson, who was particularly helpful in the early stages of its preparation; Professor Paul Wooley and Dr. Ned Stonehouse of Westminster Theological Seminary, Philadelphia; the Rev. Messrs. G. T. Williamson, Theodore J. Georgian, and Eugene W. Allen; and Mr. Fred Stone and my brother Logwood Oliver. Mr. and Mrs. Charles H. Craig were of invaluable assistance. Their suggestions have brought a number of crucial thoughts into sharper focus. My beloved wife [Ruby] deserves special mention not only for her labor in typing and retyping the manuscript, but also for her many helpful suggestions in its preparation and for patiently bearing with me during the many long hours at night and early morning spent in writing.

For any errors of judgment the writer bears the blame. Whatever praise this book may earn, the author shares with the many who have labored with him.

C. Herbert Oliver
Houlton, Maine

INTRODUCTION

Just as freedom of thought sounds the death warrant for all tyrants and dictators, so freedom of thought is breaking the bonds of racial tyranny that is so characteristic of "race relations" in the modern world. The power of free thought is clearly seen in the pages of history. The most outstanding example of this may be seen in the colossal efforts of Luther and Calvin to free the minds and souls of men from a tyranny of human inventions and unscriptural dogmas. It is to these giants of faith and action that modern democratic institutions owe their origin. The days of the tyrannies of kings and prelates were numbered when Luther nailed up the Ninety-Five Theses and when Calvin published his *Institutes*.

Genuine freedom of thought must not be thought of as the rejection of all authority save the human mind. Such a concept would mistakenly ignore divine revelation. Contrary to the profession of "free thinkers" that they represent the noblest ideals of freedom, they actually only succeed in *binding* the minds of men to purely human notions. The Christian is too often represented as being bound in his thinking, and those divorced from Christian dogmas and religion in general as being free in their thinking. But he who is bound to God is truly free, whereas he who is bound by sin is not only the most abject slave, but is ignorant of his bonds. Apart from Christian faith, freedom in this world is only illusory, as it is merely the repeated exchange of one form of bondage that fails to satisfy for another form of bondage that it vainly hopes will satisfy.

Bondage to human inventions, whether they be religious or secular, cannot calm the deepest surging of man's soul. He is indeed free who is securely bound to God the Creator, through God the Son, by God the Holy Spirit. To perceive the unfathomable love of God in redeeming sinners is the absolute ultimate of spiritual happiness, and only he who humbly receives God's grace may perceive God's love. Just as the child is most free when he is most obedient to the wise counsels of a guardian, so men are most free when they most joyfully submit themselves to the sovereign will of Him whose divine counsels are so gloriously revealed to us in the Scriptures.

I am aware that in this book there is a somewhat ambiguous use of the word *race*, due in part to the inaccurate meaning this term has popularly assumed. In an effort to avoid this unfortunate connotation, I have at times used the word *groups*, as it is not fraught with so many psychological connotations. However, at other times in a concession to popular usage I have used the term *race*.

I have also used the term *Negro*. Throughout the world this word excites a variety of emotions. Some peoples of Africa whom the West has desired to describe as "Negroes" vigorously reject the term. This attitude is normal, for what the West has historically meant by "Negro" is anything but complimentary. It is not surprising that the term is Western in origin. However, a new meaning has crept into that word. Those who have been thus historically identified have also rejected the old meaning of the word and have placed an entirely new meaning upon it. It is now a term of dignity, of manliness, of courage. It stands today as a symbol of the age old struggle for life, liberty, and the pursuit of happiness. It has not enjoyed a painless development. Nor is the title always acceptable. But history is full of examples of terms of reproach being taken by the reproached and built by their efforts into a term of dignity and irreproachableness. It is in this manner that I intend it here.

My procedure in *No Flesh Shall Glory* is as follows. First, in chapter 1 I state the basic truths of the unity of the human race. Many will take serious exception to this concept. However, I hope that instead of laying the book aside they will bear with me at least through chapters 2, 3, and 4 in which I attempt to document this position further by an appeal to and an exegesis of the Scriptures. In chapter 2 I deal expressly with biblical references to "color," and in chapters 3 and 4 discuss the significance of Shem, Ham, and Japheth. In chapter 5 I seek to show that Christian ethics and segregation are incompatible. I seek to demonstrate in chapter 6 that freedom to associate is a basic element of good human relations, and finally in chapter 7 point out that the fear of the oft-alleged consequences of non-segregation is unjustified.

It is not my intention to advocate or bolster racism of any kind, but to curtail all types of racism by destroying the ground on which they stand and by pointing men to nobler ends than race competition. Such competition has been with us for a long time and is now threatening to erupt on a worldwide scale. As a Christian my deepest sympathies lie with the claims of God and His Kingdom, which Kingdom will ever prevail over all opposition, Jew or Gentile, black or white. It is my fervent prayer that those who claim allegiance to our Lord and Savior Jesus Christ will share my conclusions as to the implications of His divine revelation in this connection.

1

THE UNITY OF THE HUMAN RACE

A MARVELOUS FACT stares each Bible reader in the face. That fact is that the human race is one. In Genesis 1:27 we read that "God created man in His own image, in the image of God created He him, male and female created he them." Throughout the Bible this great fact stands as one of the great foundational truths of revealed religion. Many have been the writers who have claimed that God created their own particular race and have assumed that other races have come from some less significant or unknown origin. But the Bible rises above such narrowness and declares in no uncertain terms that God is the Creator of all men.

But some will ask why are there such differences among people? Why are they not all alike so they could get along with each other better? Anyone who opens his eyes to see the beauties of nature will readily see that God is a God of variety. It has not pleased God to make *any* two things alike. God has created a world in which varieties are endless, and the more men increase in heavenly wisdom the more they are able to see the limitless display of God's creative genius. The God of the Bible obviously hates sin, and it is also clear that he loves variety. He has declared His hatred of sin in the Bible and by judgments upon men. He has displayed His love of variety by refusing to create any two things exactly identical. And if God loves variety, it is perverse for men to hate it.

The differences among men only reflect the love of God for variety among His creatures. God created Adam and Eve with the inherent capacity to procreate endless varieties, and as long as the world lasts these varieties will continue to appear. All the races are only crystallized varieties of men. New varieties are ever being formed as differing racial groups mingle together. In the process of time some varieties will crystallize to form new races with marked characteristics, but it should never be forgotten that they will only be varieties within the human family with the same capacity as their ancestors to contribute to the formation of new varieties.

In an age when certain men are desperately reasserting the worn-out dogmas of race superiority, the above truths are especially pertinent. It can hardly be emphasized enough that it was God who created man with the capacity to vary. Surely His purpose was not to encourage discord in diversity. To argue that God made men different in order to keep them separate is anti-Christian. The capacity to vary is a God-given capacity, inherent in the reproductive process. This should convince all men that varieties were intended by God to take place and to continue. Is it not therefore naive and perverse for one variety to consider itself a choice variety that must never change or contribute to other varieties? The symphony orchestra produces pleasing harmony not *in spite of*, but *because of* differing instruments. The *different* instruments make the symphony.

As you read this sentence, pause a moment and observe the many colors that surround you, in pictures, rugs, curtains, chairs, tablecloths; in trees, grass, earth, or sky. Think now of the beautiful rainbow or the most picturesque sunset you have ever seen. Do not these scenes fill the heart with sweet wonder? Does not the painful beauty of a sunset ravish the heart? The consistent Christian in head and heart also rejoices in the rich varieties of skin colors, for they too reveal the glory of God's handiwork.

One afternoon as I sat leisurely observing the splendor of God's creation, I was completely charmed by the intensely beautiful vestures of God's footstool. The sturdy hills, the stately trees, the clear skies, the gentle wind and the happy birds were all praising Him with their music and declaring His great glory. I saw at one glance so many varieties of vegetation that I was forced to conclude that God loves variety. Their manifold numbers were only a small reflection of the greatness of God the Creator and Redeemer. No less does He love variety among men, for from every tribe and tongue He calls His people to be a praise unto His everlasting name.

The human race is one, and all attempts to prove otherwise can only end in failure. There are many who profess to believe in the unity of the human race; however, totally unaware that to divide the indivisible is a glaring contradiction, they feel justified in maintaining that the "races" must be kept separate. Many of these are afflicted with a profound hatred, based on profound ignorance and nourished by a profound prejudice. Others are more enlightened and, desiring to be rational, point out how birds of a feather flock together. But the paucity of their defense shows the weakness of their position, for new feathers appear when birds do not fear.

Those who think in terms of separateness are guided by what we call "racial solidarity." Racial solidarity is the cohesion of a group around a few physical characteristics such as skin color, hair texture, and facial features. It seems that color ranks highest in importance, though Darwin truly called it the most fleeting of all characteristics.

The racist has one aim in view: viz., to bring about, promote, and enhance the dominant position of the "race" of which he is a member. His greatest fear is what he terms "intermarriage," because it breaks the racial solidarity of his group and threatens its dissolution. In his book *The Direction of Human Evolution*, E. G. Conklin says, "Every consideration should lead those who believe in the superiority of the white race to strive to preserve its purity and to establish and maintain the segregation of the races, for the longer this is maintained the greater the preponderance of the white race will be" (p. 53). Such is the philosophy of the racist.

As I shall seek to demonstrate, this view has had its day. It is now in the balance and is found wanting. Its chief faults are that it is anti-Christian and inhuman. It is anti-Christian in that it makes impossible genuine Christian love. It is inhuman in that it works untold harm to the so-called inferior races. It is contrary to nature, for its very life depends upon false biological distinctions that nature does not recognize. And being contrary to nature it cannot be permanent, but only a passing phase in man's history. Indeed it is dead already, for God has not promised to sustain a racist society, and what God has not promised to sustain is dead.

How does the doctrine of race solidarity fare in the light of Christian teachings? True Christianity cannot fit into the narrow mold of racial solidarity. It is too broad, too universal, too worldwide in its scope. At one time Peter held a view somewhat akin to that of the race solidarist (though his was not in the least racial, but religious), but God in a vision broke the narrow mold of Peter's outlook and gave him a worldwide view that embraced all men as one human family under God and in need of redeeming grace (Acts 10).

The promises of God have absolutely no relation to racial solidarity. Nowhere does the Bible foster the spirit of racial solidarity. True, God called Abraham and promised to make of him a great nation, but God did not have reference merely to his natural seed, but also and especially to his spiritual seed, which all believers are. "If ye be Christ's, then are ye Abraham's seed, and heirs according to the promise" (Gal. 3:29). The seed of Abraham are those about whom Peter speaks when he says, "Ye are a chosen generation, a royal priesthood, an holy nation, a peculiar people; that ye should show forth the praises of Him who hath called you out of darkness into His marvelous light" (1 Peter 2:9). The idea of racial solidarity is alien to the Bible and should be thoroughly rejected in all Christian circles. To the extent that Christians advocate, or acquiesce in, a view of racial solidarity, to that extent they fall short of the genius of Christianity. There are many Christians who strive for better race relations, but when their views of race solidarity are undisturbed, their task is necessarily frustrating.

The notion of race solidarity itself must go, for not until this notion is abandoned and Christian solidarity encouraged in its stead will genuine Christianity once again come to the fore. As racial solidarity in one group creates a reactionary racial solidarity among excluded "races," and as it requires a double system of ethics (one for the solidaric group, and one for the excluded groups) it should be easy for Christians to see the shortcomings of such a philosophy.

But alas, Christians seem to learn more slowly than the children of darkness, for the world seems to be leading the way in the battle against the dogmas of racism. The Supreme Court decision of May 17, 1954 outlawing enforced segregation in our public schools should have reflected the crystallized sentiment of the churches. But the churches have but slowly chimed their agreement with the decision, and an "integrated" church is still a novelty. Perhaps too many church members have convinced their consciences that segregation is right, and a convinced conscience is more rigid than a convinced mind. A convinced mind can be changed, but a convinced conscience is almost unmovable.

Racial solidarists do emphasize a unity. But such unity is narrow and racial and falls far short of the biblical doctrine of the unity of the whole human race. The Christianity of those, therefore, who are conditioned primarily by ideas of race falls far short of the essence of true Christianity. Such ideas are a burden to Christianity, and only as they are discarded may there arise a powerful and vigorous Christianity, before which no force in the world can stand.

Racial strife in the world today is basically due to our sinful natures. More specifically, it may be traced to the dogma of racial solidarity that prevails so widely in our time. It would be a sad mistake to think that the darker peoples of the world hate white people simply because they are white. The fury of mobs in Algeria or Hong Kong is not directed against Europeans because they are white, but because as whites they have engaged in extending their solidaric relationship and dominance to the hurt of peoples excluded from that relationship. When all the false claims to racial superiority are repudiated by all who entertain them, better human relations will be the inevitable result. True, problems will arise, but they can be solved when the basic truth of the unity of the human race is made foundational in our thought and actions.

The problems involved in "interracial marriage" are deeply involved in all that has been said about the unity of the human race. As restrictions on such unions are the last outpost of the race solidarist, and also a means by which race solidarity is protected, this question requires separate attention. We shall return to it in the sequel.

Has the doctrine of evolution succeeded in bringing

about better social relationships among human beings? One would expect that a doctrine that links organically man and the beast would have played a major role in enhancing better human relations by presenting a broad basis for better understanding between *human beings*. But no doctrine has been more successful in dividing mankind into racial camps than this doctrine of evolution. The fuel of racism is the theory of evolution. And though many racists oppose evolution, they are more under its influence than they realize.

Evolution professes to emphasize the true nobility and dignity of *man*, but in the practical outworking, it does not stress the dignity of man as such, but of a particular race of men. It labors under the psychological necessity of erecting horizontal divisions among "races" so as to demonstrate a gradual rise from lower forms to higher forms. The chief proponents of this doctrine quite naturally place themselves at the top of the process of man's development, and the "savage" at the stage next above the primates. But this view not only strikes at the very heart of the unity of the whole human race, it closes its eyes to the savagery of the "civilized." The beastly deeds of "civilized" mobs are legion. And as evolution has failed to discover the true dignity of *all* of mankind, it has failed to discover the true dignity of any *part* of mankind.

Man's true dignity lies in the fact that he was created immediately by God in His own Image in knowledge, righteousness, and holiness. All men are men by virtue of God's direct creative act, not by virtue of a development from a lower form of existence to a higher. And any view that robs man of this glory destroys the only true basis for a truly harmonious society. Evolution may provide a basis for a homogeneous society, but such a society is necessarily narrow and brittle, and far from suitable for life in a shrinking world where diverse peoples are minutes rather than months away.

The sincere Bible reader will discover a twofold solidaric relationship among men: that of all men in Adam, and of all believers in Christ. These relationships have their source in God and are unchangeable. And what God has joined together, let not man put asunder. By virtue of the former solidaric relationship all men are sinners and under the divine sentence of death. By virtue of the latter solidaric relationship all who have been ordained to eternal life shall obtain that blessedness through Christ. The racist ignores these relationships and goes about to establish the solidarity of one phase of the human family. That such solidarity is divisive, unchristian, and destructive of any genuine harmony in society should be beyond doubt. The Christian must therefore be quick to repudiate all attempts to justify a segregated society, for segregation puts asunder what God has put together.

2

THE BIBLE AND COLOR

Western Christendom assumes that civilization in general and Christianity in particular came to us from the Caucasian branch of mankind. Some have no doubts that Adam was white, or at worst a very light brown. Some writers (e.g., A. H. Sayce) have gone to great lengths to seek to prove that the Amorites, Philistines, and Libyans of antiquity were of the white race. In the past, most Bible scholars were content to concede that the Egyptians (Hamites) were black. This view was popular as long as it salved the consciences of the slave traders and slave holders, who looked upon themselves as chosen by God to fulfill a "curse" upon Ham. But when archeologists and historians discovered the greatness of the Egyptian civilization, they concluded that the Hamites were white.

In the past Negroes were looked upon as certainly the descendants of Canaan and as such were doomed to be hewers of wood and drawers of water. But when it was discovered that the Hebrew alphabet, upon which the Greek alphabet is based, was taken over from the Canaanites, adjustments had to be made and Canaanites are now looked upon as having been white. Even Toynbee has denied the existence of a black civilization in history. And to make the picture complete, some are happy to point to Simon of Cyrene (who helped Jesus bear His cross) and the Ethiopian eunuch as "Negroes."

It is my firm conviction that such representations are full of error. A thorough examination will show that truth lies in the opposite direction. Historians, biblical and otherwise, following the racial motif, have transformed the history of civilization into a history of the "Great White Race." Because this has been the case, historians free of the race motif must distinguish between actual history and biased history. People make history. The historian remakes it. And he remakes it according to the presuppositions under which he labors. Too often these premises are false. One major task of the historian, therefore, is to remove the false presuppositions of previous historians.

The Bible reader who looks out upon a world so persistently wrought up over the frivolous characteristic of color asks himself, "What does the Bible have to say about color?" Does the Bible ever associate black skin with a curse? Can we determine from the Bible the origin of the colors of men? Though these questions are largely overlooked today, a right understanding of them will go a long way toward the removal of misunderstandings about color.

The attempt to interpret blackness in terms of a divine curse is most prominent in the Book of Mormon. The Lamanites (who existed only in Joseph Smith's imagination) are said to have been turned black because of their sin (2 Nephi 5:20–25; Alma 3:6–19; Mormon 5:15; 1 Nephi 12:23; Jacob 3:5). Here we find color prejudice incorporated into a religion.

In answering the question "Do the Scriptures ever associate black with a curse?" the sincere careful Bible student must state emphatically, "No." While it is true that a curse was placed upon Canaan, no mention whatsoever is made of color. That curse was fulfilled when the children of Israel conquered and subjugated the Canaanites thousands of years ago. Moreover, the Israelites never looked upon the curse as involving color. Perhaps the reason was that they themselves were dark. Taking the Bible alone, it is easier by far to assume that the Israelites were a dark or black people rather than white, and this casts no unfavorable reflections upon those who are white. We can say with certainty that if the Israelites were white, they said nothing about it, for there is no reference whatever in the Bible to normal white skin. On the other hand, there are references and circumstances that point to the conclusion that the peoples of biblical times were preponderantly dark skinned. This does not, of course, turn the Bible into a black man's book, but merely frees it from the assumption that it is a white man's book. Neither civilization nor the Bible can be claimed by any one branch of mankind.

The names of certain Bible characters give some clues as to the skin color of certain peoples. The name *Ham* means dark, swarthy, black. In Scripture the land of Egypt is called the land of Ham (Pss. 105:23, 27; 106:22). Cush, the son of Ham was the father of the Ethiopians, a black people, and prominent throughout the Bible. Xenophanes described the Ethiopians as "black and snub-nosed." When Jeremiah said "Can the Ethiopian change his skin or the leopard his spots?" (Jer. 13:23), it was not the prophet's intention to cast an unfavorable reflection upon the handiwork of God, but simply to use the permanence of pigmentation or natural color as an illustration of the permanence of sin in the children of Israel, from which sin they could not extricate themselves. Kedar (one of the sons of Ishmael) means "black skinned." Here we have the names of three biblical characters whose skin was black and whose descendants figure prominently in the Bible. And in no instance is the color black disparaged, nor any other color for that matter, nor is any color favored. The recent attempt of certain scholars to explain Noah's naming of Ham not after his skin color but after the black soil of the

Nile is not acceptable, especially in the light of the fact that we have no evidence that Noah ever saw the Nile.

As it is now beyond question that Ham and his descendants were black, what are we to say about his immediate brothers Shem and Japheth? It is safe to assume that they too were at least dark, though men for centuries have thought and still think the contrary. The attempt to explain the naming of Ham as calculated to distinguish him as a minority must fail, as a study of the genealogy of Genesis 10 will show the Hamites to be by far in the majority and the Japhethites by far in the minority. The promise of God to *enlarge* Japheth is added confirmation of this view.

There is another factor that lends weight to the conclusion that Shem and Japheth were dark. When the brothers of Joseph went to Egypt for food because of a famine, they were not able to recognize their brother Joseph but thought he was an Egyptian. Had the Egyptians and Shemites been distinct in color, we might expect that Joseph might have been at least suspected, but his brothers never suspected Joseph of being any other than an Egyptian. Similarly Moses was thought to be an Egyptian by the daughters of the priest of Midian when Moses helped them water their father's flock and protected them from the shepherds who were molesting them (Ex. 2:16–19).

But if the above be true, how could it come to pass that so-called Japhethites (a term to be discussed more fully in chapter 4), classifying themselves as white, could find so many disparaging things about blacks in the Bible? In reality such things are not found in the Bible but have their origin in racist imaginations. Why is sin called black when Scripture speaks of it as red (Isa. 1:18)? Why do so many theological books and writings of a biblical nature disparage black? As much as I like Bunyan's *Holy War* I see no good reason why he depicted the devil, Diabolus, as king of the blacks; nor why he should make the three boys born to Mr. Vile-Affection and Mrs. Carnal-Lust black boys, naming them "Impudent," "Black-mouth," and "Hate Reproof." Why does Hengstenberg in his *Christology of the Old Testament* say that "even the name Ham, i.e., 'the blackish one,' may be connected with the character which he . . . displays" (Vol. I, p. 24)? The very suggestion is a pernicious perversion of Scripture—a reading into Scripture of the modern race motif.

Why does Catherine Vos in her *Child's Story Bible* place a black scowl on the face of Cain, while Abel lies white and still on the ground?

The Caucasianizing tendency of Oursler's *The Greatest Story Ever Told* is quite evident. Though the New Testament does not describe the eyes, hair, or complexion of its subjects, Oursler's book has an abundance of such details. According to him, Joseph has blue eyes and Mary has dark hair, a pale face, and blue eyes (p. 9). On page 119, the same Mary has dark eyes. Annas has blue eyes (p. 20) and the baby Jesus' face was white (p. 70). Herod, oddly enough, he makes dark brown and dun-skinned (pp. 82–91). Jesus was given dark eyes, brown hair, and skin paler than that of most men (pp. 114, 119). John the Baptist receives a pale face and bronze arms, while it was a red-headed woman who dried Jesus' feet with her hair (p. 194).

My point in bringing out the above is not to ridicule Fulton Oursler but to point to a rather common practice that creates false impressions. These false impressions become dangerous when Oursler goes on to describe Judas as red-headed with small black eyes and tough ringlets of hair (pp. 298, 306). At the trial of Jesus, the hired disturbers had dark faces (p. 326). The mobs around Jesus had swarthy faces (p. 352). Pilate was quite a creature. He had blue eyes (p. 357), swarthy hands (p. 358), dark eyes, and brown wavy hair (p. 353), and black hairs on the back of his hand (p. 371). The book is at its worst when Oursler speaks of a "negrillo" with apelike arms who brings Pilate a basin (p. 371). Such imaginary descriptions are fruitful of a highly distorted view of Christianity. Written into this popular best-seller is the sinister view that dark faces bespeak evil deeds while blue eyes bespeak sweet innocence. The Bible should not be so misunderstood. This type of thinking is very prevalent in Western Christendom and may be found most anywhere. Many similar examples could be cited but space demands that the above citations suffice.

I am not able to determine the origin of the attitudes reflected in the above descriptions, but the translators of the King James Version of the Bible did much to make permanent such attitudes by their translation of Song of Solomon 1:5. It reads "I am black, *but* comely, O ye daughters of Jerusalem, as the tents of Kedar, as the curtains of Solomon" (italics mine). And ever since, Western Christendom has taken an apologetic attitude toward black. A dark person is either "intelligent but dark," or "dark but intelligent," or "beautiful but black," or "black but beautiful." Such is indeed an unhealthy and an unscriptural attitude. We cannot praise the King James translators for placing a "but" where an "and" should have been. The phrase should read "I am black and comely." The little "and" makes a very great difference.

The Hebrew conjunction *vau* may mean either "but" or "and," the context determining which is proper. The Shulamite woman who speaks in verse 5 was speaking of her beauty when she said "I am black and comely" and not in any apologetic vein, for she goes on to compare her beauty with the dwellings of Kedar, the black-skinned son of Ishmael and progenitor of the people called by that name. She compares her beauty with the black curtains of Solomon that perhaps hung in the temple. But the strongest argument in favor of the use of "and" is that the Septuagint translates the Hebrew *vau* as "and." The Septuagint was a translation of the Old Testament into Greek more than two hundred years before Christ when color was no issue. And as there are two separate words in Greek for "and" (καί) and "but" (ἀλλά), the use of καί in the Septuagint places the matter beyond dispute. Unfortunately the latest translation of the Bible (RSV) by men who have a reputation for being most liberal, has retained the old-fashioned inaccurate translation of the Authorized Version. Western civilization has thrived so much from racial injustice that change is not easy; however, Western civilization was shaken to its very foundations by nothing other than Nazism, a home-grown variety of racism. And we would do well to ponder this indication of God's judgment.

The Bible towers above racism as high as the heavens are above the earth. But too often Christianity has been made to serve racial ends. Too often Western Christianity has been made either the active servant of Western imperialism or its passive defender, both of which are destructive of genuine Christian ethics.

He who would profess the one true religion, Christianity, must acknowledge the existence of one God who has revealed Himself in the Bible, and of one human race of many varieties ever changing and never static, and of one Savior whose blood makes pure and spotless the greatest sinners. And the true Christian does not flee to the Bible to confirm his prejudice, but he allows the pure Word of God to purge away his prejudices as well as his sins.

Let it be once for all settled, then, that the Bible nowhere associates the color black with a curse. Let it also be borne in mind that many peoples of biblical times may from the Bible be identified as black. And while the Bible does not identify any peoples of antiquity as white, a gross error is made when the Bible is claimed as a white or black man's book, for in the Bible the color of a man's skin is never an issue.

A further point must needs be discussed before leaving the topic of color. Throughout the English-speaking world, the word *fair* has come to mean white skin. Many Bible commentators so use the word. In his *Bible Encyclopedia and Dictionary* Faussett, following Gesenius, gives the meaning of Japheth as "to be fair," "from the fair complexion of Japheth and his descendants" (p. 328). As the word *fair* is frequently used in the English Bible, many conclude that the reference is to whiteness of skin. Recently this view has been enhanced by the writings of Yigael Yadin of Jerusalem's Hebrew University. From pseudo-Genesis scrolls he translates passages that make Sarah, the wife of Abraham, exceeding white; also, the body of Noah is described as being white as snow. The former translation is incorrect. The Hebrew word means "beauty" rather than "white," and is so translated in the scrolls a few lines below the above reference. The latter representation of Noah is purely imaginary. Such translations are in the writer's estimation weighted with far reaching political consequences as far as Western support of the Israeli state is concerned.

Biblical evidence does not in the least support the above representation. On the contrary, it supports the opposite point of view, if anything. The Hebrew word for *fair* is never used in the Bible to refer to skin color. Rather it refers to beauty, comeliness. And that the word *fair* is not used in the Bible to refer to white skin is unquestionably clear from a reading of the Song of Solomon. In 1:15 Solomon describes his love saying, "Thou art fair, my love; behold, thou art fair; thou hast dove's eyes." And his love in verse 16 describes him in similar terms, "Behold, thou art fair, my beloved, yea pleasant." Again in 4:1 Solomon says "Behold thou art fair, my love; behold thou art fair." In verse 7 he continues "Thou art all fair, my love; there is no spot in thee" (cf. also 1:8; 2:10; 5:9; 6:1; 7:6). In all these the reference is to the unspeakable beauty of one who described herself as "black and comely" (1:5), as the tents of Kedar and as the curtains of Solomon. And it is the same Hebrew word that is used to describe the beauty of Sarah. This should establish the fact that *fair* in the Bible is not used to designate skin color, but beauty.

Returning to the subject of the Egyptians of antiquity, if the reader still doubts that they were a black-skinned people, the unquestionably unbiased testimony of the light-complexioned "father of history," Herodotus, should settle the matter once and for all. In Book 2 of his celebrated *History* he tells of the conquests of Sesostris, one of the great Egyptian kings. This king, Herodotus tells us, traversed the whole continent of Asia (Asia Minor to us) "whence he passed on into Europe, and made himself master of Scythia and of Thrace" (p. 114, Rawlinson translation). On his return to Egypt a great number of soldiers for some reason remained in what is called Colchis. Herodotus continues,

> There can be no doubt that the Colchians are an Egyptian race. Before I heard any mention of the fact from others, I had remarked it myself. After the thought had struck me, I made inquiries on the subject both in Colchis and in Egypt, and I found that the Colchians had a more distinct recollection of the Egyptians than the Egyptians had of them. Still the Egyptians said that they believed the Colchians to be descended from the army of Sesostris. My own conjectures were founded, first, on the fact that they are *black-skinned and have woolly hair*, which certainly amounts to but little, since several other nations are so too; but further and more especially, on the circumstance that the Colchians, the Egyptians, and the Ethiopians, are the

> only nations who have practiced circumcision from the earliest times. (pp. 114–15, italics mine)

As a passing argument to prove that the Colchians were of Egyptian origin, Herodotus states that they were black-skinned and had woolly hair. And he casually adds that several other nations were the same. This statement stands as impregnable as Gibraltar against all attempts to classify the Hamites as white. But the surprise of the modern reader is yet to come. If he will consult his maps of ancient nations, he will find that the Colchians inhabited that land between the Caspian and Black Seas through which the Caucasus Mountains run (see p. 183). This is the area that is reputed to be the place of origin of the Caucasians or whites. There are other similar proofs from Herodotus, but this will suffice.

3

THE SIGNIFICANCE OF SHEM, HAM, AND JAPHETH

In the Old Testament we learn that there were two worlds, the old and the new. The old world had its beginning with Adam and Eve in the garden of Eden. They were upright and holy and walked in obedience to God, until in opposition to His commandment they sought material prosperity without depending upon God. The forbidden fruit seemed to promise a kind of food, pleasure, and knowledge that would elevate them to the plane of deity. But to their eternal dismay they succeeded only in plunging themselves into the abyss of sin and transgression, and into that misery that is identical with the loss of fellowship with God. The pace of wickedness and rebellion having been set by Cain, the old world became so utterly sinful that God in judgment washed it away with the flood.

The family of Noah, however, was saved from the disaster, and his three sons Shem, Ham, and Japheth became the progenitors of the new world. They were all blood brothers, born to the same parents, and each having his own wife. What is the significance of these three persons? Were they the originators of three separate races? If so, what are they? And what shall we say to the fact that they were blood brothers? How can we explain when the blood brother relationship ended and the "race" relationship began? Do the facts of the Bible bear out the view that three sharply divided races sprung from these three persons? Or does the Bible continue throughout to deal with men as one human race?

To these questions we will direct our thoughts in this chapter. We shall discuss the views found in various Bible commentaries relating to Shem, Ham and Japheth. We shall seek to show how modern racist attitudes have been read into the ancient biblical account. Then in chapter 4 we shall consider the biblical history itself, tracing the descendants of Shem, Ham, and Japheth from the biblical account. We shall seek to discover whether the Bible regards them as the progenitors of three separate races destined to remain divided on the face of the earth or whether it regards them simply as members of the one human race without racial divisions being erected between them.

There are almost as many views of Genesis 9:25–27 as there are individuals. Everyone has his own view of what was involved in the curse upon Canaan and what part, if any, Shem and Japheth play in the curse. The purpose of the present chapter is to present in brief compass the views of a variety of well-known Bible commentators. There are a number of commentators who read modern history back into these verses. There are other commentators who, following the rule of interpreting Scripture by Scripture, have set forth a more accurate view. We will deal with the former commentators first. The reader should consult the Bible and keep these verses before him while reading this chapter. Each of the following comments is confined to an interpretation of these verses.

Keil and Delitzsch. In their commentary on Genesis, Keil and Delitzsch say "In the sin of Ham 'there lies the great stain of the whole Hamitic race, whose chief characteristic is sexual sin' and the curse which Noah pronounced upon this sin still rests upon the race." The enclosed quotation was taken from Ziegler, another Bible commentator. Keil and Delitzsch falsely classify the Phoenicians, Carthaginians, and Egyptians as belonging to the family of Canaan. But Canaan was the grandson of Ham, the father of the Egyptians. True, the Phoenicians and Carthaginians were Canaanites, but it is more accurate to classify all as Hamitic rather than Canaanite. These commentators also classify the Persians, Macedonians, and Romans as Japhetic, and make them the subjugators of all of the Hamitic families down to the present.

A brief reading of the imprecation of Noah, however, will reveal that only the Canaanites are to be subjugated, and they were to be subjugated not to Japheth but to Shem. This subjugation was carried out thousands of years ago when David broke the power of all the Canaanites and put them under tribute. Reading into this the curse of modern slavery (which Keil and Delitzsch do not hesitate to do) is a gross misrepresentation of the Bible. Such commentators fail to realize that even the descendants of Shem, whom God had promised blessings to the enrichment of the world, were bondslaves to Ham in Egypt for over four hundred years, and were delivered from such bondage not by their own might but by the power of God.

George Bush. In his *Notes on Genesis*, Bush says that the curse affected the descendants of Ham as well as the Canaanites, citing as evidence "the fate of the African race" (p. 163). Thus he reads modern history into an ancient prediction long ago fulfilled. He does, however, call attention to the fact that Melchizedek, after whom Jesus Christ is a priest forever, and Rahab, one of the natural progenitors of the Son of God, were Canaanites. God's mercy is not like that of men. Men exalt themselves as the predestined executors of the will of God in history only to fall into utter ruin after a season of false prosperity.

J. G. Murphy. In his *Commentary on the Book of Genesis* Murphy also takes the position that the curse on Canaan is punitive of all the Hamitic races. He says, "In modern times it is well known that most of the nations of Europe trade in African slaves" (p. 212), and he cites this slave trade as confirmation of a biblical curse upon Hamitic races.

Jacobus. In his *Notes on Genesis* Jacobus says the curse covers the descendants of Ham, pointing to the modern enslavement of the Negro as evidence (p. 195).

Arthur Pink. In his *Gleanings in Genesis* Pink says, "The curse was not confined to Canaan but embraced all the descendants of Ham" (p. 125). He says further that it is well known that the "Negroes who were for so long the slaves of Europeans and Americans, also claim Ham as their progenitor" (p. 126).

Matthew Henry Commentary. Though Henry does not extend the curse to all the descendants of Ham, yet he says that the birthright was divided between Shem and Japheth, Ham being utterly discarded. But such a representation simply is not to be found in Scripture.

Jamieson, Fausset, and Brown Critical and Explanatory Commentary. This popular volume simply states as facts that "this doom has been fulfilled in the destruction of the Canaanites—in the degradation of Egypt and the slavery of the Africans, the descendants of Ham."

Butler's Bible Work. In this work J. G. Butler departs from Scripture interpretation and enters the field of race propaganda. He says, "On Ham, and mainly on Canaan, the curse of slavery is to press." He says that there is foretold in this oracle a threefold development of humanity: (1) the redemption race of Shem, (2) the heroic and cultural race of Japheth, and (3) "a third for its ungodliness will bear the curse of history, subjected and enslaved by its brethren, laden with the world's ban." But such is not the judgment of God, but Butler's own misjudgment. Perhaps he had not read of the degradations that Paul condemns in Romans 1, which gross sins are according to Butler's theory attributable to the cultured Japhetic Romans. Perhaps he did not realize that Greek and Roman culture borrowed heavily from the Egyptian civilization. Further, Butler closed his eyes to the fact that the cultures that come under consideration in the Bible are largely Hamitic. And if Butler was too small to pay tribute to the greatness of ancient Egypt, one greater than Butler was not too small. For Tacitus says that "the Egyptians were the first who had the ingenuity to express by outward signs the ideas passing in the mind. . . . Their hieroglyphics were wrought in stone and are to be seen at this day, the most venerable monuments of human memory" (*Annals*, Vol. 2, Book 11).

Matthew Poole. In his *Annotations on the Bible* Poole says, "When Canaan is mentioned, Ham is not exempted from the curse, but rather plunged into it" (p. 25).

G. F. Oehler. Oehler's monumental work on *Old Testament Theology* includes an extensive but most misleading comment on Genesis 9:25–27. He says, "The words of Noah in Genesis 9:25–27 are of the greatest importance for the conception of the general history of mankind given in the Old Testament." He extends the curse to Ham. Curiously enough he seems to find evidence for dividing the human race into two camps, those who are to be receivers of divine blessings, and those who are the enemies of God (p. 56). But did any people rage more against the church than the Romans? And many prophetic teachers today tell us that the spirit of anti-Christ is to proceed from Gog, a Japhethite. The distinctions which Oehler makes are false and very misleading. Sin is not racial; nor is righteousness. We should bear in mind that some of God's worst judgments have been poured out upon those who ignore their own sinfulness and at the same time lay claim to divine blessings on the basis of racial traits.

James Comper Gray. In his *The Biblical Museum* Gray quotes Dean Alford saying that "The curse, as a matter of world-history, has more or less followed all the Hamite races" (p. 45).

The Preacher's Homiletic Commentary. This work, edited by Exell and Leale, quotes many commentators and concludes that the curse embraces Ham.

On the particular point under discussion, the above writers provide their readers with a host of errors, and any generation nourished on such misrepresentations is certain to have faulty ideas of the Bible and race. It is my contention that the curse upon Canaan was upon Canaan and his descendants and was fulfilled when the children of Israel overcame the Canaanites as we read in the book of Joshua. The curse was completed under David who subdued the most fierce of the Canaanite tribes, the Philistines. Yet it is most significant that David did not for once claim that he was fulfilling the curse of

Noah upon Canaan. His one aim was to vindicate the honor of God, not to establish his racial integrity as of a higher caliber than that of the Canaanites.

We now turn to some commentators who, when speaking of the passage under consideration, belong in a different category.

Ryle Cambridge Bible Series. In his *Genesis* Ryle says, regarding Genesis 9:25–27, "There is no suggestion of a whole race doomed to a condition of slavery. The application of this clause to the African races is an error of interpretation" (p. 128).

Leupold. In his *Exposition of Genesis* (pp. 349–50), Leupold says, "To hold that this word (speaking of the curse) broods like a dark and inescapable fate over the future of a race, is to hold a very grievous misunderstanding." He holds that Noah was simply stating a prophecy that the moral guilt of Ham would express itself in Canaan and his descendants. It was this writer who suggested the position that I now embrace—that the subjection of the Canaanites is seen in the conquest of Canaan by Israel. However, I do not share his view that the curse includes the subjugation of Carthage. Noah simply does not say enough for us to extend the prophecy to Carthage. It seems that those who insist on extending the curse to Carthage and all Africa, are motivated by a desire to establish a point that has racial value for those who promulgate the view. Such a motive is necessarily at variance with the spirit of the Bible. It rather fosters that detestable racial pride that thrives on misrepresentation. The Christian must rise above such sinful motives and let God alone be his glory. And when God is our glory we do not need the props of racial achievement to bolster our pride.

Robert S. Candlish. In his *Book of Genesis* Candlish says that the curse is only upon Canaan and not upon the descendants of Ham (p. 125). It was fulfilled when the children of Israel went into the land of Canaan. However, like Leupold, Candlish extends the curse to the Carthaginians who were descendants of Canaan. His reason was that the Romans needed to subdue all the world for the fast spread of the gospel, and Carthage stood in the way. But Rome itself, rather than preparing for the fast spread of the gospel, actually stood in the way of the gospel. The gospel spread in spite of and not because of Rome.

H. B. Pratt. Pratt tells us in his *Studies on the Book of Genesis* that the curse did not fall on Ham but only on Canaan. He correctly adds that it "had nothing whatsoever to do with the Africans (whom alone some persons would see in this prophecy) but with an Asiatic race—the Canaanites, whose land was taken from them and given to the descendants of Abraham; and the remnants of them, those who remained in the country, were reduced to a form of slavery." He continues, "It is therefore an inexcusable error and an unjustifiable and hurtful misinterpretation of prophecy to infer from the sin of Ham and the curse pronounced upon Canaan, that from ancient times God has consigned the African to perpetual servitude" (pp. 117–18).

Marcus Dods. In his commentary on Genesis Dods says, "The fulfillment of the curse must not be looked for in the other descendants of Ham, and still less in the Negro races" (p. 44).

J. P. Lange Commentary on Genesis. Lange's comment on the passage in view is as follows: "Before all things we must hold fast to this, that the language of Noah is an actual prophecy;

and not merely an expression of personal feeling. That the question has nothing to do with personal feeling is evident from the fact, that Ham was not personally cursed" (p. 337).

Bishop Ellicott. In his commentary on Genesis Bishop Ellicott has this most revealing comment on the so-called Hamitic curse. "So far from Ham being accursed, his descendants were building mighty cities, such as Egyptian Thebes, Nineveh, and Babylon, were rearing palaces, digging canals, organizing governments, and founding empires at a time when the descendants of Japheth were wandering over Europe with no better weapons than implements of flint and bone. The application of the curse to Ham seems to have been suggested to commentators by the degradation of the African race in modern times, and especially the prevalence of Negro slavery: but anciently the converse was the case, and for centuries the Egyptians, a Hamite race, made the Israelites serve them" (p. 145).

It is to be regretted that most Western minds have followed the erroneous racial interpretations of this passage rather than the correct interpretations of an Ellicott or a Lange.

It should now be beyond doubt that the Hamites were black and that from them great civilizations have come and passed. Hence, the darkness with which the so-called Japhethites have obscured Hamitic civilizations should be removed.

With the passing of slavery there came a lessening of emphasis upon a biblical curse upon Hamites and African people. Only the ignorant and obstinate continue to espouse such views. But there has come in the place of such views another equally erroneous view, that the Hamites were white. When the spade of archaeology revealed the marvels of ancient Hamite civilization, scholars could not concede that they belonged to the black family, and a new rereading of modern history into ancient history took place.

In the *Jewish Encyclopedia*, Vol. 5 (p. 55), we are told that "Egypt . . . formed a branch of the great white African or Hamitic family." We have already stated the conclusion of Toynbee. J. H. Breasted in his *Ancient Times: A History of the Early World* extends the Great White Race to include Hamites and all civilization. In Hammond's *Illustrated Library World Atlas* (p. 275), we are given the conclusion of anthropologists that "The Hamites who inhabit north and northeast Africa, belong to the Caucasian branch of mankind."

Writers like A. H. Sayce and Sir. H. Rawlinson have done much to foster the erroneous view that the ancient civilizations were white, and most of their evidence is extremely trivial. For instance, Sayce argues from the height of the Anakim (of which Goliath was a representative) that they must have been white (cf. his *The Hittites*, p. 16). The conclusions of these and other similar writers certainly suggest that their aim is simply to establish the whiteness of peoples of ancient civilizations, a motive that is indeed prejudiced. Such a motive cannot lead one to true history, but merely to history reconstructed after the image of the prejudiced historian.

Evidence of the falsification of history by Sayce may be seen in his comments on an ancient Babylonian prayer. The prayer, addressed to Bel Merodach, a god of ancient Babylon, reads, "The merciful one, with whom is the giving of life, may his word be established, and not forgotten, in the mouth of the black-headed ones, whom his hands have made." The Babylonian word "Adam," meaning "man" was used by the Babylonians of themselves. Yet Sayce says that the Adamites of the old Babylonian legends were the white race of Semitic descent (cf. his *Fresh Light from the Ancient Monuments*, p. 27).

His explanation is that a so-called white Semitic race overran the black-heads and called themselves Adamites. At best this makes the biblical account a usurpation of an originally black culture, but Sayce passed over the difficulty in silence. And only the racist mind of Sir H. Rawlinson could find a parallel between "The dark and white races" of Babylonia and the "sons of God" and the "daughters of men" of Genesis.

The attempt to rob the black man of his history must utterly fail as it is not founded in fact. Happily, C. W. Ceram in his book *The Secret of the Hittites* avoids the racist error. Speaking of ancient Hittites he says that we are not linked to them by ties of race (p. 71), a welcome word from one who vindicates much of the writings of Sayce. In the same book there is a statement well worth quoting as it goes to the heart of this discourse. Ceram quotes Winckler, an outstanding German archaeologist, as saying, "Civilized peoples are never racially pure; rather they are always the product of a large number of strata formed by more or less different races" (p. 50). Such words are especially refreshing in our day when racism is again rearing its ugly head. Inconsistently, however, Ceram includes the Hamites in the white race (p. 77).

The Christian historian must be guided by a higher motive than race. He must see the earth as the Lord's and the fullness thereof, the world and they that dwell therein. To narrow the world down to the possession of a race is to perpetuate the age-old strife of men. God has consistently frustrated all peoples and nations who have with blind and sinful hearts laid claim to that which is rightly His. And He changeth not. Only the Christian faith has the framework for universal harmony among peoples. Let the Christian rise to the occasion today and make practical the great doctrines of the Bible, which truths alone can transcend the narrow bounds of race.

In the last few centuries a great deal of emphasis has been placed upon the significance of Shem, Ham, and Japheth, the three sons of Noah from whom the earth was repopulated after the flood. Unfortunately most of the emphasis has been racial and has been productive of bitter fruit. We shall presently discuss these three characters with the purpose of tracing their activity and discovering their biblical destiny.

4

THE BIBLICAL HISTORY OF SHEM, HAM, AND JAPHETH

Japheth. In Genesis 10 we are given the genealogy of Japheth, Ham, and Shem. We will discuss them in that order. The first thing we learn about Japheth is that he was smaller than either Shem or Ham in descendants. This gives point to the words of Noah that God shall enlarge Japheth. Many commentators interpret the phrase "and he shall dwell in the tents of Shem," as referring to Jew and Gentile enjoying the blessings of salvation, or dwelling together in harmony. Many commentators even exclude Ham from all heavenly blessings, e.g., Matthew Henry, but the error is obvious. The blessings of salvation are for all who believe, whatever may be their tribe, tongue, or nation. Further, Jew-Gentile relationships in history contradict any notion of harmony. Also the enlargement of Japheth would make it quite impossible for him to dwell in the tents of Shem. The most intelligible explanation of this phrase is that it is God who is to dwell in the tents of Shem. All difficulties are overcome when we realize how God chose Shem to dwell with him and to bless the nations with salvation through a descendant of Shem, Jesus Christ.

The view that it is Japheth who is to dwell in the tents of Shem may have some plausibility especially from a study of

Isaiah 49 and 54. In Isaiah 49 the isles are called upon to hearken to what God would do for his chosen people. If these of the isles are Japhethites, then it would seem that Isaiah perhaps had in mind the prophecy concerning Japheth in Genesis 10:5. In Isaiah 49:6 God says he will give Israel for a light to the nations, and in verses 19 and 20 there is a necessity for the enlargement of Israel to accommodate the nations that came to them. The nations are in need of a larger place in which to dwell. And in Isaiah 54:2 the prophet, dealing with the same subject, says, "Enlarge the place of thy tent . . . for thou shalt break forth on the right hand and on the left; and thy seed shall inherit the nations." We may be sure that the prophet is speaking of the spiritual light that the nations will enjoy through receiving the gospel of salvation. This light is to proceed from God's chosen people; but more especially from God's righteous Servant, the Messiah, Jesus Christ.

Yet in spite of these factors, it seems to me to be more in accord with Scripture to say that God rather than Japheth is to dwell in the tents of Shem. Commenting on this point in the *International Critical Commentary* (p. 186), Skinner says, "The older view, which explains Shem and Japheth in terms of the Table of Nations, i.e., as corresponding roughly to what we call Semitic and Aryan races, has always had difficulty in discovering a historic situation combining Japhetic dominion over the Canaanites with a dwelling of Japheth in the tents of Shem."

The descendants of Shem are Gomer, Magog, Madai, Javan, Tubal, Meshech, and Tiras. Gomer is mentioned only in chronologies, except in Ezekiel 38:6 where the bands of Gomer are referred to. That prophecy is one of judgment against Gomer. His sons were Ashkenaz, Riphath, and Togarmah. In Jeremiah 51:27 we learn that Ashkenaz had a kingdom. Riphath is mentioned only in chronology. In Ezekiel 27:14 we learn that Togarmah traded with Tyre; and in Jeremiah 38:6 we read of God's judgment upon his descendants. In Ezekiel 38 and 39 we have the awful prophecy of the destruction of Magog and Gog. The last earthly judgment of God is to be upon Gog and Magog (Rev. 20:8).

Madai is mentioned only in chronology, though the Medes are said to have been descended from him. If this is so, then Madai and his descendants gave birth to a powerful kingdom, but it was destroyed by God.

Javan, the fourth son of Japheth, along with other Gentiles are to see the glory of God (Isa. 66:19). Also Javan traded with Tyre (Ezek. 27:13, 19). The Greeks are said to have descended from Javan. The sons of Javan were Elishah, Tarshish, Kittim, and Dodanim. While Kittim and Dodanim are mentioned only in chronology, Elishah is said to have traded with Tyre (Ezek. 27:7). Tarshish is frequently mentioned. The ships of Tarshish brought Solomon gold, silver, ivory, apes, and peacocks (1 Kings 10:22); Jehoshaphat sent the ships of Tarshish to Ophir for gold (1 Kings 22:48; 2 Chron. 9:21); Tarshish was much affected by the fall of Tyre (Isa. 23:1, 6, 10, 14; Ezek. 27:12, 25). It was to Tarshish that Jonah sought to go while fleeing from God. This great maritime people, however, was brought low by judgment from God (Isa. 2:16). The next son of Japheth, Tubal, traded with Tyre (Ezek. 27:13); is seen by Ezekiel in hell (Ezek. 32:26); is to feel the judgment of God (Ezek. 38:2; 39:1); and is also to see the glory of God (Isa. 66:19). Meshech also traded with Tyre (Ezek. 27:13); is seen in hell (Ezek. 32:26); is judged by God (Ezek. 38:2, 3; 39:1). A psalmist cries in despair that he sojourned as a captive in Meshech and in Kedar (Ps. 120:5). Tiras is mentioned only in chronology.

From the above references we have a picture of the descendants of Japheth, who they were, what they did, and what befell or is to befall them. Some references were omitted to avoid repetition. One fact of particular significance is that the descendants of Japheth depended heavily on Tyre for trade, and the destruction of Tyre must have spread havoc in the distant isles.

Before we leave Japheth we must discuss Genesis 10:5, in which we read, "By these were the isles of the Gentiles divided in their lands." Does this mean that the Gentiles are to be identified with the Japhethites? Many commentators have made this error and have consequently run contrary to biblical teaching. The Gentiles are simply the nations. This name was given them before the Israelites became a nation for the purpose of distinguishing those whom God had chosen for a saving purpose from the nations, all of which worshiped idol gods. And after the Israelites became a nation, they continued to speak of the Gentiles, not only to distinguish their worship of the true God from all idolatry, but also to foretell the mercies of God that the Gentiles would receive through Christ. The very promise that God gave Abraham, separating him from all unbelief, included most emphatically all the nations of the earth. In calling Abraham, God's purpose was not to establish an elite and inherently righteous nation (for both Testaments condemn the Israelites for being just the opposite) but to use him as a means of granting saving mercies to all nations. This promise was fulfilled by the perfect life and substitutionary death of Jesus Christ. In the great commission Jesus sent out the apostles to preach the gospel to all nations, and those who receive it are the true seed of Abraham.

The term *Gentiles*, therefore, is not rightly restricted to Japhethites. In Jeremiah 25:15–26 the Gentiles are Egypt, Philistia, Edom, Moab, Tyre, Zidon, Arabia, Elam, Medes, etc. Hamites are included as well as Japhethites. In Jeremiah 46:1 an extensive prophecy against the Gentiles commences with Egypt, and continues against Philistia, Moab, Ammon,

Edom, Damascus, Kedar, Hazar, Elam, Babylon. Notice that the judgment is against the Gentiles, yet no mention is made of Japhethites. Acts 7:45 should put the question beyond dispute, as there the Canaanites are described as Gentiles. The term *Gentiles*, therefore, is inclusive of both Hamites and Japhethites. It may be used with reference either to Hamites or Japhethites or both, depending on what the writer has in view. And in Genesis 10:5 the isles are in view. The Japhethites are simply the Gentiles who inhabited the isles.

Another fact that comes forth from a study of what the Bible has to say about the descendants of Japheth is that the Japhethites are consistently referred to as being far away from the center of God's redemptive activity. Such expressions as "afar off," "from afar," and "the isles" in reference to the descendants of Japheth seem to point to this conclusion. In Isaiah 49:1 we read "Listen, *O isles*, unto me, and hearken, ye people, *from far*." Likewise in Isaiah 66:19 we read of Tubal, Javan, and the isles afar off. Jeremiah 25:22 speaks of the *isles beyond the sea* (Mediterranean), which to the Israelites must have been far away. In Jeremiah 2:10 we read of the isles of Chittim, or Kittim, the son of Javan. Jeremiah 31:10 reads, "Hear ye the word of the Lord, O ye nations, and declare it in the *isles afar off*." Other references are Esther 10:1–2; Psalm 72:10; Isaiah 23:6; 42:4; 60:9; Ezekiel 26:15, 18; 27:3, 6, 7, 15; 39:6; Zephaniah 2:11. And in the New Testament there is Acts 22:21, where Jesus said to Paul, "Depart: for I will send thee *far hence* unto the nations." Certainly this must mean that the Japhethites were to be turned from darkness to the light of the gospel. The isles that waited for God's law were to receive it through God's wonderful mercy. In preceding ages they had been the remotest from the influences of God's law and from His people. And Paul labored northward and westward bearing the message of hope to the lost sons of Japheth.

Of course it would be a great error to conclude from the above that this mercy is exclusively for the descendants of Japheth. Nothing is more contrary to Scripture, for there are many passages that speak of the blessing of redemption as coming upon the sons of Ham; for example Isaiah 19:21, 25 and Psalm 68:31. Further the term *nations* or *Gentiles* includes not only Hamites and Japhethites, but also other descendants of Shem who were not among the chosen seed; for example, Elam, a son of Shem, in Scripture refers to Persia. In Acts 2:9 the Elamites are mentioned alongside many others who heard the gospel at Pentecost. Lud and Aram, sons of Shem, also come under the classification of "Gentiles" because it was not through them that the promised seed of the woman was to come. It was through Arphaxad, the third son of Shem, that the chosen people came. The other descendants developed into nations, but they were not the chosen ones. In fact, in the whole genealogy of Jesus Christ we notice that one son of many was chosen by God as the one through whom the promised Messiah was to come.

We have seen that according to Bible representations the Japhethites occupied the distant islands, and were farthest removed from the cradle of civilizations in Egypt and Mesopotamia. The Bible has nothing whatsoever to say about the color of Japheth or any of his descendants. Nor is there found any clue in the Bible that may help one in determining the color of Japheth. To conclude that he was white is an unwarranted assumption. The silence of the Bible in this matter should make us conclude that color is of no importance whatever in God's dealings with men. Therefore scholars who seek to discover color conflicts in ancient history do irreparable damage to the cause of good human relations. Actually racism is a modern, not an ancient, concept. Equally blameworthy are the scholars who claim the cream of ancient civilizations to have been white. Such historical racism has turned many capable historians from the path of true history.

Ham. In 1 Chronicles 4:40 we read of the inhabitants of Gedor, that the land was fat with pasture and good, wide, quiet and peaceful; "for they of Ham had dwelt there." Other specific references to Ham are found in Psalms 78:51; 105:23, 27; 106:22. These passages identify Egypt with the land of Ham. The sons of Ham were Cush, Mizraim, Phut, and Canaan. The descendants of these sons were spread abroad in Africa and the Near East: Cush in Ethiopia, Mizraim in Egypt, Phut in Libya, and Canaan in what now comprises Palestine and Mesopotamia. In his *Analytical Concordance* Young tells us that Cush means "black." In Genesis 10:8 we are told that Cush begat Nimrod. The account lingers with Nimrod and we read that he began to be a mighty one in the earth, that he was a mighty hunter before the Lord, that the beginning of his kingdom was Babel, and Erech, and Accad, and Calneh, in the land of Shinar. Also out of the land of Shinar Nimrod went forth into Assyria and built Nineveh, Rehobath, Calah, and Resin, a great city. From this description we see that the Cushites were a mighty people with many great kingdoms. The Cushites (or Ethiopians) are mentioned repeatedly in the Bible. The dispersed Israelites are to be gathered from Cush (Isa. 11:11). God speaks judgment upon Cush (Isa. 18:1). Ethiopia is to stretch out her hands to God (Ps. 68:31). A river from the garden of Eden encompassed the whole land of Cush. The Greeks called the Cushites Ethiopians, which means "burnt face." I see no reason why the Greeks should be accused of a color racism because of this title. It was not given in a spirit of disdain, nor taken by the Cushites as an insult. A modern example of the same thing is the term "paleface" applied by the Indians to the white man. The only difference is that the term "paleface" is not a national name.

There are many references in the Bible to judgment upon the Cushites. In Numbers 12:1 we read that Moses married a Cushite woman. In 2 Chronicles 14 Ethiopia is smitten by Asa, king of Judah. Isaiah 20:4 predicts the fall of Ethiopia and Egypt to Assyria.

The sons of Cush as given in Genesis 10 are Seba, Havilah, Sabtah, Raamah, Sabtecha, and the mighty Nimrod. Seba is mentioned again in Psalm 72:10 and Isaiah 43:3. In the first reference Sheba and Seba, along with the kings of Tarshish and of the isles, are to offer gifts to the Messiah. Havilah is mentioned in Genesis 2:11; 25:18; and 1 Samuel 15:7. From these references we may conclude that Havilah did represent a kingdom. Sabtah is mentioned only in Genesis 10, though it was likely a part of Arabia. Raamah traded with Tyre (Ezek. 27:22) and had two sons, Sheba and Dedan. From Sheba there came a nation, and a famous queen who visited Solomon and exchanged gifts with him. Sabtecha is mentioned only in the genealogy under consideration. The last son of Cush was Nimrod, and by far the greatest. The great nations of antiquity Babylon and Assyria were built by Nimrod. Genesis 10:11 appears to read that Asshur built Nineveh. However the marginal reading seems to be more correct. In it we see the reading "out of that land he went forth to Assyria and built Nineveh." This would mean that out of the land of Shinar Nimrod went forth and built Nineveh. This view is supported by Micah 5:6, where Assyria is called the land of Nimrod.

A word now must be said about the land of Shinar. The evidence of Scripture supports the conclusion that the land of Shinar is the same as Babylonia. The tower of Babel was built in the land of Shinar (Gen. 11:2). A remnant of dispersed Jews are to be gathered from Shinar (Isa. 11:11). When the children of Israel were captured by the Babylonians under Nebuchadnezzar and were taken to Babylon, Daniel 1:2 says they were taken into the land of Shinar. And in Zechariah 5:11 we read that a house is to be built in the land of Shinar, but the meaning of this is not clear to the writer.

We have now proceeded to the place where we can look back and make a revealing observation. We have seen that Babylon and Assyria were Hamitic. It is also clear from the Bible that Assyria captured and removed the northern tribes of Israel, and Babylon carried Judah into captivity. In the light of these facts it is most absurd to hold that the curse upon Canaan included all Hamites. On the contrary, God used Hamites to carry his own people into captivity that they might see the folly of idolatry. Isaiah 11:11 is full of meaning in this connection. The prophet there speaks of the fact that God will again bring his people out of captivity saying, "And it shall come to pass in that day, that the Lord shall set his hand again the second time to recover the remnant of his people, which shall be left, from Egypt, and from Pathros, and from Cush, and from Elam, and from Shinar, and from Hamath, and from the islands of the sea." All of the places where the Israelites are held captive are Hamite, except Elam, which was Shemite, and the islands of the sea, which were Japhetic.

The second son of Ham was Mizraim, which means Egypt. In the Bible there are by far more references to Egypt than to any other country. The greatness of the Egyptian civilization is common knowledge to all, and because of this greatness various historians, for racial reasons, wish to classify it as a white civilization. This desire is understandable when one realizes the majesty of ancient Mizraim. But the humbling of Egypt in antiquity should make all historians aware of the profound truth that God brings down to the dust all nations that do not worship the one true and living God, self-revealed in the Bible. The descendants of Mizraim are Ludim, Anamim, Lehabim, Naphtuhim, Pathrusim, Casluhim (out of whom came Philistim), and Caphtorim. The Lehabim were perhaps the ancient Libyans. The Philistines of Canaan descended from the Casluhim, and are also associated with the Caphtorim (cf. Jer. 47:14; Amos 9:7). It is speculated that the name of the Caphtorim is preserved in the name of the ancient Egyptian city Coptus.

The third son of Ham, Phut, does not beget a number of nations, but only he himself becomes a nation. Many identify Phut with Libya, as also Ludim. In certain verses of the Bible Phut is translated Libya (cf. Jer. 46:9; Ezek. 30:5; 38:5). Other references to Phut are Ezekiel 27:10 and Nahum 3:9.

The fourth and last son of Ham, Canaan, begat a great many nations. We shall discuss each one briefly. Sidon, the firstborn, founded the great city Sidon with which the sister city Tyre is associated in antiquity. This ancient Phoenician city was most noted for its skill in woodcraft. Solomon seeking help from Hiram in the building of the temple acknowledged to him that "there is not among us any that can skill to hew timber like unto the Sidonians" (1 Kings 5:6). Speaking of ancient Sidon Jesus said that if the mighty works had been done in it as had been done in Chorazin and Bethsaida, it would have repented in sackcloth and ashes long ago (Matt. 11:21). The second born son of Canaan, Heth, is said to be the progenitor of the Hittites. Much is being written today about the Hittites and one of the problems among scholars in this field is that of the identity of the Hittites. The conclusion of some, that they were Indo-European, is not acceptable.

The fact that the Hittites are repeatedly mentioned alongside other Canaanite tribes in the Bible points to a Canaanite origin of the Hittites. The desire to Caucasianize the Hittites has led to the unacceptable conclusion that the Hittites were Indo-European. Unfortunately he who relies upon biblical evidence is considered unscholarly. But were it not for biblical evidence, the Hittites would have been utterly lost to history. There is a passage that *may* imply that the Hittites were not Canaanite. In Genesis 23:10 we read that Ephron the Hittite dwelt among the children of Heth. One might get the impression that a Hittite, distinct from the children of Heth, negotiated the sale of a piece of land for Abraham to bury Sarah. Yet the evidence is not conclusive. The listing of the Hittites among the Canaanites so consistently in the Bible establishes the conclusion that they were a Canaanite people. They need not have been restricted to the land of Canaan, but their origin is undoubtedly Hamito-Canaanite. The Jebusites dwelt in and around Jebus, which ultimately became Jerusalem. David fought against the Jebusites and subjugated them (2 Sam. 5:7–9). The Amorites were one of the most powerful Canaanite tribes. They were tall and strong (Amos 2:9–10) yet they were destroyed by the Israelites and their remnant subjugated by Solomon (1 Kings 9:20–21). The Amorites were also the most wicked of the Canaanite tribes, and when their iniquity was full, God destroyed them by means of the children of Israel. But in time Israel herself, to her everlasting shame, fell even lower morally than the Amorites (2 Kings 21:11) and God punished them by delivering them over into captivity. The Girgashites, Hivites, Arkites, Sinites, Arvadites, and Zemarites all experienced the fate of the other tribes. Only Hamath was not subjected to the Israelites, as the northern border of Israel was at the entering in of Hamath (cf. Num. 34:8; 1 Kings 8:65). Hamath was, however, conquered by the Assyrians (2 Kings 18:34; Isa. 10:9).

It is clear from Scripture that the prophetic curse on Canaan was fulfilled in the subjection of the descendants of Canaan to the descendants of Shem. When the Israelites were preparing to cross the river Jordan and enter the land of Canaan, God encouraged Joshua with these words, which Joshua also spoke to the people: "Hereby ye shall know that the living God is among you, and that He will without fail drive out from before you the Canaanites, and the Hittites, and the Hivites, and the Perizzites, and the Girgashites, and the Amorites, and the Jebusites" (Josh. 3:10). After the capture of Ai, the Canaanite kings united against their common foe Israel. They are listed in Joshua 9:1 as the Hittite, and the Amorite, the Canaanite, the Perizzite, the Hivite, and the Jebusite. Throughout the book of Joshua the central theme is the struggle of the Israelites with the Canaanites in the land of Canaan. The Israelites were victorious, but they did not drive out the Canaanites. Rather they dwelt together with them and were so influenced by them as to be led into idolatry. This was most displeasing to God, and He delivered them time and again into the hands of various Canaanite kings, and when they called upon Him He sent them a judge to deliver them. The book of Judges tells of the ups and downs of Israel in the land of Canaan. It was not until the time of David that the last remnant of the Canaanites (the Philistines) was defeated and made servants. And under David the prophecy of the subjection of Canaan received its fulfillment. To extend the curse over all Hamites, or to extend it into modern times, or to attempt to bring Japheth into the particular Canaanite prophecy, is not only historically false, but a dangerous perversion of Scripture.

From this study of Canaan and his descendants we see the fulfillment of the prophecy of Noah. The Canaanites were subjected to the Israelites and were eventually destroyed. Also from the study of all the descendants of Ham we see that most of the great civilizations of antiquity were Hamite. Egypt, Babylon, Accad, Assyria, Ethiopia, Libya, Tyre, Philistia, Phoenicia, and many others sprang from Ham. We find also that there is no evidence whatsoever for a Hamitic curse. And it need hardly be said that nowhere in the Bible is there the faintest suggestion of a curse attached to black skin. And if any reader still persists in the view that it does, let him study the judgment of Miriam.

Shem. In the beginning of Shem's genealogy we are told that he was the father of all the children of Eber. Since the word *Hebrew* is a variation of the Hebrew word *Eber*, it is likely that the Hebrews derived their name from Eber. We find the name of Eber only in chronological tables in the Bible, except in Numbers 24:24 where Balaam prophesied that ships from the coasts of Chittim would afflict Asshur and Eber (both Shemites) and he would perish forever. The children of Abraham, however, who also called themselves Hebrews, were not destined to such a fate.

The children of Shem were Elam, Asshur, Arphaxad, Lud, and Aram. The descendants of Elam built Persia, a great nation, with Shushan as its capital. In Isaiah 21:2 the prophet sees the fall of Babylon under the sword of Elam and Media (the Medes and the Persians). And Daniel 8:2 states that Shushan was in the province of Elam. And in Acts 2:9 we read that there were at Jerusalem on the day of Pentecost Medes and Elamites. Shushan means "lily" and "white." Hebrew variations of Shushan mean "white marble" or "white fine linen." A descendant of Anak was named Sheshai (white) (Num. 13:22). A man named Shashai is mentioned in Ezra 10:40. And in 1 Chronicles 2:31, 34, 35 one of the children of Israel was named Sheshan. These names are all variations of the Hebrew word meaning white. But it is far from certain that there is any reference in these names to white skin. And if it does refer to white skin, we may be certain that such a title was not worn as a badge of superiority, else Sheshan would not have given his daughter to wife to Jarha his Egyptian servant (1 Chron. 2:35).

Asshur's descendants are not given in Genesis 10, nor

are the descendants of Lud. The Lydians of Asia Minor and of North Africa may have sprung from Lud. The descendants of Aram were Uz, Hul, Gether, and Mash. The land of Uz was the home of Job (Job 1:1). There were kings in Uz against whom Jeremiah prophesied (Jer. 25:20). Hul, Gether, and Mash are listed only in chronological tables in the Bible. The descendants of Arphaxad are dealt with in more detail, as it was through this son of Shem that Abraham, David, and the Messiah were to come. Arphaxad begat Salah, who is mentioned only in chronological tables. Salah begat Eber, whom we have discussed above. Eber begat Peleg, who was living when the earth was divided into linguistic groups. Eber begat also Joktan, who begat thirteen sons, most of whom are mentioned only in chronological tables. They settled in southeast Arabia. At the end of the genealogy of Genesis 10 we read, "These are the families of the sons of Noah, after their generations, in their nations: and by these were the nations divided in the earth after the flood."

We have now surveyed the biblical treatment of the sons of Noah. The discerning Bible reader will notice that Genesis 10 is a basic chapter in understanding what the Old Testament says about nations and peoples. Time and again we meet in the Old Testament with the descendants of Shem, Ham, and Japheth as given in Genesis 10. In Ezekiel 27 the descendants of all three sons are discussed in relation to the fall of Tyre. Let the reader now turn to that chapter and read it making special note of the many references to Shemites, Hamites, and Japhethites.

What conclusions can we now draw from the biblical facts we have been considering? There are at least two profound truths that come to us, truths that are full of meaning today in a world torn by racial and national strife.

First, we may confidently state that the treatment of the sons of Noah was *not* designed to institute and perpetrate permanent national or racial divisions among the children of men. The unity of the human race is nowhere jeopardized. Nowhere does the Bible place these sons in three separate opposing camps. Rather the Bible is full of evidence of the crossing over of the general lines delineated in Genesis 10. There were political alliances among all three as well as economic cooperation (Ezekiel 27 confirms this). Blessings and curses are pronounced upon all three. Among all three are those who by God's grace are to become partakers of the Abrahamic covenant of eternal life through the promised Messiah. The Bible draws no marriage lines between any of the three sons or their descendants, except for religious purposes. God's people were forbidden to marry idolaters lest their faith be corrupted. But beyond this the Bible erects no barrier. Moses marries an Ethiopian woman. Joseph marries an Egyptian woman and begets Ephraim and Manasseh by her. It was considered a distinctive achievement for Solomon to have a daughter of Pharaoh as his wife. Rahab the Canaanite marries Salmon and gives birth to Boaz, the father of Obed, the father of Jesse, the father of David, from whose loins sprung the Savior, Jesus Christ (Matt. 1:5). Indeed almost all the postdiluvian women of the Bible were either Hamites or Shemites. The Japhethite nations had not yet been enlarged and therefore had not attained world significance. It is most unfortunate, however, that so-called Japhethites have in modern days built around themselves a racial barrier beyond which they are not supposed to trespass, and into which no one outside the limits of their definition of the "white race" may peaceably come.

A second conclusion that we may draw from the study of the sons of Noah is that no significance whatsoever is attached to skin color. The variety of skin colors among men is a gift of God built into the very nature and constitution of man. Such variety cannot be eliminated because it is God-ordained. And it is wicked and perverse for men to despise what God has ordained, whatever it may be. Let no racist, therefore, appeal to the Bible in support of his notions, for the Bible condemns him. Those historians who reconstruct ancient history on a racial basis are among the greatest obstacles to the improvement of human relations in the world today since they provide what to the uninformed seems a sound basis for discrimination.

But how may better human relations be attained in a world in which unchristian and inhuman concepts of "race" have become so entrenched and frozen as to express themselves in policies such as segregation in the United States and apartheid as in South Africa? To what extent may these systems be condoned? What does the future hold for such systems? However serious and earnest may be the efforts of men to perpetuate racial separateness, such separateness is an unnatural relationship; it has never succeeded, and it is doomed to failure in God's world. God has frustrated all the false hopes of nations of antiquity, and all hopes of power based on racial solidarity are now being frustrated and will ultimately be destroyed by the Almighty God. Until men learn to glory in the great name of the one true God, the God who has revealed Himself in the Bible, and in His glorious Son Jesus Christ, their false hopes will be laid in the dust. History cries aloud this truth. The Bible shouts it more plainly. Let peoples and nations today hear and understand. Policies of separateness can succeed only as the segregated group is kept in ignorance and economic weakness. And is it Christian to impose ignorance and poverty upon *anyone*? The growth of intelligence and economic strength among the separated group brings with it an outward rejection of their imposed status that inwardly they had rejected all along. We cannot justify anyone who cannot find love in his heart for that which is made in the very image of God Almighty, and all men are made in that image. We cannot justify a system that in any way detracts from this great truth, and all segregated systems detract from this great truth. Among such systems, however, there are those who rise above their narrow and perverted surroundings and make unforgettable footprints in the sands of time. We cannot forget a General Lee who did not scruple to kneel with his black brother to receive the communion of the body and blood of our Lord Jesus Christ. We cannot forget the humble Lincoln, ever looking forward on the lowly penny to a better day in human relations. Though these men were not completely free of the racism of their day, they rise so high above the masses of their time as to deserve perpetual and warm memory. We cannot forget a Justice Ware, or a Father Huddleston, whose love of justice exceeded by far their love of position. And there is the kind word or deed of one neighbor to another, of black to white or white to black, which never reaches the ears of the many, which are passed over in silence by the multitudes, but which an all-seeing God never forgets.

Is there a way out of the dilemma of modern racism? We shall seek to find an answer in the succeeding chapters.

5

CHRISTIAN ETHICS AND SEGREGATION

THE TASK OF ethics is to discover what is right and wrong. There are many systems of ethics, each of which has a basic starting point and ultimate goal all its own. There is the ethics of hedonism that asserts that pleasure is the only real good. Within the framework of hedonism stands the egoist, who considers only his own pleasure; the altruist, who seeks first the well-being of others; and the utilitarian, who seeks the greatest happiness of the greatest number. There is the idealistic ethics, which rejects pleasure as the only good and places supreme value upon a certain kind of character directed toward either self-realization as an individual, or social self-realization, in which case the state is given first consideration. There is the ethics of evolution, which asserts that whatever contributes to the survival of the species is right, and whatever endangers the species or impedes the process of evolution is wrong. The ethics that justifies segregation fall into this category.

Whatever the segregationist and evolutionist consider a threat to their survival causes them great alarm. The person who thinks primarily in terms of survival and extinction will naturally react violently against what seems to him to portend his own destruction. Hence, the segregationist faces a real dilemma. However, it is a dilemma created on the false platform of his own making, a profound prejudice of which he is not even aware.

Unfortunately many Christians betray the genius of Christianity by subscribing to a system of ethics that cannot be reconciled with Christianity. Christian ethics is to be distinguished from the above, and all other systems. While it is not basically a system of pleasure, in contrast to the shallow and fleeting pleasures of the hedonists, it recognizes that the only source of the deepest and most lasting pleasure is in commitment to Jesus Christ as Lord and Savior. While its end is not mere self-realization, in contrast to the selfish and temporal aspirations of the idealist, it provides for the fullest realization of the self in time and in eternity. For in God, through Christ, the Christian has pleasures forever more. And only he who loses his life through faith in Christ may find it again, full, rich, and complete. For in Christ dwells all the fulness of the Godhead bodily, and Christians are complete in Him.

Historic Christian ethics is authoritative to the core. It rests not upon human authority of either church, state or custom, but wholly upon the Scriptures, the only infallible rule of faith and practice. Man's chief end is neither pleasure, nor self-realization, nor survival; it is to glorify God and to enjoy Him forever. The alpha and omega of Christian ethics is the glory of God, the God who has revealed Himself clearly and sufficiently in the Bible. The chief concern of Christian ethics is to *know* and to *do* the will of God as revealed in His Word. But lest faith be lost sight of, let us bear in mind the words of Jesus in John 6:29: "This is the work of God, that ye believe on Him whom He hath sent." Christian ethics is not detachable from faith in Christ. And being inseparably bound to faith in Christ as the wondrously glorious Savior from sin through

His atoning blood, Christian ethics is grounded in the revealed will of God for conduct among men. The Bible reveals how Christians should act toward Christians and toward non-Christians. One word, *love*, sums it all up. While the Christian should have a special love toward other Christians because they are "blood" brothers, bought by the precious blood of Christ, he should never forget that, as Jesus taught in the parable of the good Samaritan, all men are our neighbors. When this truth is taken seriously, it strikes a deadly blow at the heart of all social distinctions. All such distinctions are basically artificial and have no permanent place in the kingdom of God.

The aspirations of the natural man may be summed up by the words *wealth* and *culture*, *prestige* and *power*. All too often in this world, ill-gotten gains are employed to enhance the fame, culture, and political advantage of their possessors. And the story of history is the story of the acquisition and the loss of these advantages. The Christian, however, has riches far beyond the reach of thieves, moth, or rust; riches not ill-gotten, but purchased by the precious blood of Christ; riches that intensely satisfy the hungry soul in this present vale of tears; riches that have an eternity in which to reveal their glories; riches of the assurance of God's love, of the knowledge of sins so costly, and yet so freely forgiven in Christ, of eternal fellowship with God the Father, Son and Holy Spirit. He who has these blessings has all things. And he who has not these blessings, though he "own" the earth, has nothing. Obviously then, social distinctions based on material possessions employed to glorify man rather than God are artificial and violate Christian ethics. Christian ethics has a higher standard of value, and to this standard all Christians should strive to conform. This does not mean that a Christian cannot have earthly riches. Abraham was a very wealthy man. But the fact that he had an absolute faith in God, and did not trust in his wealth for security, is of greatest importance in understanding his greatness. Though he was rich, his security was not his wealth, but God. Job was a man of great wealth, but that his confidence was not in riches is seen in that when he had lost all his wealth, he still blessed the name of God. What an astounding thing to bless the name of God in calamity! And what a wonderful confirmation of the fact that the Christian is governed by a heavenly code of ethics!

Christian ethics is based squarely upon the Ten Commandments. These commandments stand as a monument to remind all men of the high requirements of God. They are God's absolute standard of conduct for men, to which all men are bound to conform if they would have fellowship with a righteous God. In both Old and New Testaments the Ten Commandments stand as the law of God for men who would be holy, just and good. The error of the Pharisees was that they thought they kept the law of God, while in reality they were the greatest hypocrites. They could not acknowledge that "all have sinned and come short of the glory of God." Rather they went about to establish their own righteousness, which in the sight of a holy God was only filthy rags. The righteousness that God requires has been perfectly performed by Christ, and it is His righteousness, received by faith, which justifies the believer in the sight of God.

When these truths are taken seriously, it becomes obvious that Christian ethics cannot support segregationist ideas, for such ideas have no place whatsoever in a truly Christian view of life. Nowhere in the Bible is the slightest suggestion that people are to be separated purely for racial reasons. In principle segregation is anti-Christian, for it severs bonds that God has created. In the natural realm God made only one race, the human race, and all people are bound together by virtue of this creative act of God. In the spiritual realm God bestows his saving mercies upon those of every race, nation, tribe, or tongue. His blessings are not distributed by race or nation, but to all who receive His promises and rest in the finished work of Christ. Segregated churches are therefore diametrically opposed to the Christian ethic they profess to teach. Likewise all organizations that by terms of admission are inclusive of only one "race," or that exclude any "race," cannot rightly enjoy the title of Christian. This does not mean that the Christian does not have the right to choose his friends. The reasons for his choice, however, should be in accord with Christian ethics. To exclude any individual from one's circle of friends or acquaintances for purely racial reasons can hardly be called Christian. Too often those racists who protest that their right to choose their friends is endangered when segregation is rejected, fail to realize that those whom they would exclude have an equal right to choose their own friends. And we should also realize that we do not have the right to decide directly or indirectly whom others should choose for their friends or with whom others should associate. Segregation implies such a right.

A complete system of segregation can hardly prevail in a land where Christian teachings are accepted. As segregation is basically inhuman and unnatural, a thoroughgoing system of absolute segregation throws all morality and decency to the wind in its dealing with the segregated group. It is hard to understand how a conscience even remotely influenced by Christian teachings can do this. The segregationist who wishes to improve the intelligence and educational standards of a segregated group is also faced with a painful dilemma, for education and segregation cannot be blended; they are mutually exclusive. Where enlightenment thrives, segregation cannot stand. Where segregation is most complete, intellectual growth is most effectively crushed.

The Bible assumes the unity of the whole human race. And because of such unity the gospel is applicable to all men without distinction of race, nationality, or language. However, it should not be necessary to elaborate on individual passages of Scripture that bear on this particular subject. The burden of proof rests upon those who deny what the Bible clearly teaches. They must advance biblical passages that contradict these facts. This, we contend, they are unable to do.

A change-over from a segregated society to a non-segregated society is not easily accomplished. Such a change should be based on enlightened Christian ethics, for only then may the results be good and lasting. The strife that characterizes all major social, political, economic, and religious changes will even more characterize a change from a segregated to a non-segregated society, for such a change involves all four of the above phases of life. At the root of such a situation lies the relative inability of institutions to change so as to adjust properly to new conditions. Institutions have their source in ideas, and ideas have always been slow to change, and more so institutions. Why so? The ideas that are expressed in institutions are not easily arrived at, and therefore not easily changed. Ideas easily acquired are easily lost. When ideas become expressed in institutions, such institutions represent a great abundance of planning, toil, and labor. And as institutions are thought by their contemporaries to embody all the wisdom of the past, resistance to change is understandable.

We must have institutions, however, and we should try to make them as permanent as possible. Yet the permanence of these institutions makes them defy change, and they refuse to give ground without a struggle. Thus, when men seek to insure the welfare of their posterity by setting up institutions, they only prepare that which change will take away. For new conditions will inevitably arise calling for institutional changes, which, as we have seen, are not accomplished easily. Thus arises the problem of stability and progress. There cannot be progress without stability, nor stability without progress. A society must be stable in order to make genuine progress. A ship that is to sail from one island to another can hardly make progress if the islands are sailing too. A society that is truly stable must not be static. It must make progress. The ideal society must have a stable, permanent element as well as a progressive changing element. Most societies tend toward a static, fossilized existence, and thus become brittle and fragile and incapable of defense from threats from within or without.

Indeed the framers of the Constitution were men of great wisdom in that they erected a system of government that is both stable and progressive. Its stability is seen in the fact that it has outlasted any system of constitutional government devised by man. Its progressiveness is seen in the fact that the Constitution survived a changeover from an agrarian society to an industrial society. The status of millions of our inhabitants has been radically altered for the better without the writing of a new constitution. Even the profound changes wrought by a civil war left the Constitution intact and as strong as ever. And while we hail these changes as in accord with the spirit of the Constitution, we cannot agree with those who represent these changes as not in agreement with the original intent of the framers of the Constitution. Such an attitude reflects the static tendency in society. It would require all generations subsequent to that of the framers of the Constitution to fashion their lives and institutions according to the original intent of the framers of the Constitution. But our forefathers would have been the first to reject this notion. They would certainly expect their posterity to evaluate their original intent in the light of future developments in the life of the nation and the world.

With the recent decisions of the Supreme Court affecting so profoundly social life in the United States there is no danger in the foreseeable future that American society will degenerate into a fossilized society. That danger is more acute in a homogeneous society.

The best system that history affords of a society in which social and economic forces were not allowed to degenerate into a fossilized state was that system that Moses under divine inspiration gave to the children of Israel. And the one factor that contributed most to the maintenance of a fluid society was the year of Jubilee. In that year all property was returned to its original possessor, thus preventing a class from being expropriated. In that year all persons who previously had to sell themselves because of debts were to be set free, thus preventing the growth of a class of hopeless poor. And an unfortunate who became a servant by debt and whose fortunes changed before the year of Jubilee could purchase his freedom by calculating the value of his services up to the next year of Jubilee. Thus the year of Jubilee, which came every fifty years, tended to prevent that exploitation and expropriation so prevalent in surrounding nations.

Since Christianity not only embodies the kind and merciful spirit of the Mosaic economy, but improves upon it immensely, the effect of the Mosaic economy, and more, is obtainable: where Christianity abounds and is taken seriously.

Is it not begging the question to seek to justify a fossilized, segregated caste system on Christian principles? It is a logical impossibility, and a source of frustration to all who try.

A constant source of irritation in any segregated society arises from the necessity of classifying the segregated group. In South Africa classifications have been made according to hair texture, the folly of which will become proverbial. Ethics is deeply involved in such a procedure and only a fool could maintain that such a procedure is in accord with Christian ethics. In this country, certain states have made laws defining a Negro as one who has one-sixteenth or one-eighth Negro blood. The arbitrariness of such laws, and of attitudes in sympathy with them where no such laws exist, is evident to the casual observer. Painful indeed have been the experiences of those who all their lives have considered themselves white only to find that somewhere along the line there is a drop or two of "Negro" blood. May the day for those experiences soon be past forever in American society! I have used the term *"Negro" blood*, which in spite of the declarations of Christianity and the findings of science will not down. Actually blood is not distinguishable by race. But if one drop of "Negro" blood makes a white person a Negro, then by all laws of logic, one drop of "white" blood would make a Negro white. But as the segregationist has a logic all his own, the force of this argument does not impress him. How rightly has Gunnar Myrdal pointed out that the word *Negro* is a social, not a biological concept (*An American Dilemma*, p. 136). The heathen notions of the superiority of blood or of physical characteristics, must give way before the Christian concept that God made man in His own image. And only those who reflect that image in knowledge, righteousness, and holiness have reason to rejoice. Yet their rejoicing is not in themselves but in God.

There seems to prevail a universal tendency among men to look down upon others. The psychological makeup of men seems to require that they have someone to look down upon. This attitude was *not* built into the nature and constitution of man, but it is the result of sin. It reflects a depraved nature. Only in the Christian religion is there a genuine remedy for such an attitude. The Christian does not labor under the psychological necessity of looking down upon any fellow human beings. For the true Christian sees himself before God as at the bottom of the ladder, utterly destitute of all goodness Save in the goodness of Christ. Though Paul could have boasted of his superiority over Gentiles, or even over other Jews (Phil. 3), he chose to count all earthly advantages but dung, that he might win Christ. He saw himself as the chief of sinners and unworthy to be called an apostle. The Christian whose conscience is smitten because of the knowledge of his own sinfulness can hardly find room in his heart for an attitude that disdains others.

It is my most sincere prayer that all those who are called by the name of Christ may cast aside the evolutionary ethics of segregation and embrace the noble and humane ethics of the Christian faith and thus prepare the way for relationships among men that are truly to the glory and honor of the one true God.

The hard facts, however, are that men are still like the builders of the ancient tower of Babel, whose aim was the preservation of their own name rather than the name of God.

The proponents of segregation, it must be admitted, are not at a loss when it comes to conjuring up arguments in favor of segregation. But it should be clear that all their arguments are plagued with a basic inescapable inconsistency. They propound the high ideals of individual freedom on the one hand, and on the other hand they defend their freedom to curtail the freedom of others. This basic inconsistency is an integral part of the American historical process, but it is by no means beyond remedy. Astounding progress has been made, and the future promises more progress.

As a people we Americans have relied heavily on the counsels of great minds. When we think of liberty there are at least two great men who come to mind: namely, Thomas Jefferson and Abraham Lincoln. The Declaration of Independence is saturated with the unquenchable fire of liberty in the exercise of inalienable rights. We feel the heat of death-defying conviction when Jefferson wrote "We hold these truths to be self-evident, that all men are created equal, that they are endowed by their Creator with certain inalienable rights, that among these are life, liberty, and the pursuit of happiness." And Lincoln, with the fierceness of subdued and controlled rage, appealed to these same words to cauterize the notion that slavery exists by divine right. In his second inaugural address he says ironically, "It may seem strange that any men should dare to ask a just God's assistance in wringing their bread from the sweat of other men's faces." Liberty takes courage when such stalwarts vouch for her, but how long can she be oppressed?

There is another side of Jefferson and Lincoln that is often overlooked by the champions of good human relations. In his very late years Jefferson wrote, "Nothing is more certainly written in the book of fate than that these people are to be free; nor is it less certain that the two races, equally free cannot live in the same government. Nature, habit, opinion, have drawn indelible lines of distinction between them." And Lincoln in his debates with Douglas clarified his position on the Negro in the following words: "I will say then that I am not, nor ever have been, in favor of bringing about in any way the social and political equality of the white and black races; that I am not, nor ever have been, in favor of making voters or jurors of Negroes, nor of qualifying them to hold office, nor to intermarry with white people; and I will say, in addition to this, that there is a physical difference between the white and black races that I believe will forever forbid the two races living together on terms of social and political equality."

We might well ask "What was that physical difference?" and "How could Lincoln speak so knowingly about it?"

May the good that Jefferson and Lincoln have spoken live long. May the evil of their statements above lie interred in their bones. For if blacks and whites cannot live together peacefully under one government, they cannot live peacefully in one world. A world divided against itself cannot stand. I do not expect either blacks or whites to be permanently removed from the earth, for both are wonderful creations of God. I do expect that the world will cease to be divided into color camps. Our liberties must not be abandoned; yet unless they are shared they will be lost. To the many noble words of Jefferson and Lincoln we may readily and heartily agree. But to their expressions of a prejudice that we know today to be wrong, we must reply unhesitatingly, "Get thee behind me, Satan." The honesty of Lincoln is not in the least challenged by this attitude, for he spoke as honestly as did Peter when he rebuked his Lord and master when he spoke of His crucifixion. But he was not aware of his inconsistency in advocating an unequal equality. Jefferson and Lincoln were grappling with problems of the greatest magnitude, and they could labor only with the tools they had at hand. It is true that they had the Bible, but prejudice blinded their eyes to the full light of the Bible. They could clearly see some of the implications of a profession of Christianity, but they could not see far enough. In our age when the implications of Christianity are more clearly seen in all areas of life, it does us no honor to return to the prejudice and bitterness of a bygone age. The more robust the Christian faith, the more effect it will have on all matters of social relationships and in all areas of life. We should be wiser today than we were yesterday.

Today much is made of the doctrine of original intent. The desegregation decision of the Supreme Court is opposed by many because it is said to be in violation of the original intent of the framers of the Constitution, and of the framers of the fourteenth amendment. The purpose of this argument, however, is not so much to defend the Constitution as it is to defend the status quo. It is without doubt that the Supreme Court decision banning the reading of the Bible in public schools was contrary to the original intent of the framers of the Constitution. It was certainly contrary to the original intent of Horace Mann. Yet that decision, the worst consequences of which are yet to be felt, was received with comparative quiet. *And even if it were conceded that the desegregation decision were contrary to the original intent of the framers of the constitution, yet if they were living today, being the intelligent men they were, they would frame their concept of justice and liberty in the light of twentieth century developments, rather than in the shade of ancient prejudices.* The decision of May 17, 1954 simply granted to all citizens of the United States of America the privileges and immunities that the Constitution guarantees to all the citizens of the United States. An amendment to the Constitution is therefore quite unnecessary in order for citizens to enjoy the privileges and immunities guaranteed them by the Constitution.

Before leaving this chapter a word must be said concerning the Dred Scott decision of the Supreme Court in 1857, one of the most controversial decisions ever handed down by that tribunal. In the Lincoln-Douglas debates Lincoln tried with all his might to shake loose the implications of that decision from the firm teeth of Douglas, but without success. That decision brought to light a serious oversight on the part of the framers of the Constitution. They had failed to determine precisely what a citizen of the United States was. I believe the Constitution did include free Negroes in the phrase "free persons" (Art. I, Section 2, paragraph 3); and that the Dred

Scott decision was unconstitutional in denying full citizenship to those upon whom the Constitution had conferred it. For there were free Negroes in the land before the Constitution was framed, and they must have been included in the term "free persons." The decision professed to confine itself to those persons of African descent who were brought here and sold as slaves, and all their descendants who may have been emancipated, or born to any emancipated persons. But this does not cover all Africans, for some were free before the framing of the Constitution and could not constitutionally be declared not citizens. But according to the Dred Scott decision, such free Negroes or their descendants would lose their constitutional privileges and immunities if they should enter a slave state. Such is unthinkable! The decision was right in stating that the *slaves* were not citizens in the sense that the term is used in the Constitution. But the decision goes beyond the Constitution and declares that *all* persons of African descent are not included in the meaning of the term *citizen*.

But the unconstitutionality of the Dred Scott decision is put beyond question by the following quotations. That decision says that a person "may have all of the rights and privileges of the citizen of a state, and yet not be entitled to the rights and privileges of a citizen in any other state." But Article IV, Section 2 of the Constitution reads, "The citizens of each state shall be entitled to all privileges and immunities of citizens in the several states." The Dred Scott decision argues that a state may confer citizenship on a person, but such citizenship would not entitle the person to the privileges and immunities of any other state. But the Constitution is clear in stating that citizens of each state are entitled to the privileges and immunities of citizens in the several states. (The passage of the fourteenth amendment nullified the Dred Scott decision forever.) It was argued that at the time of the framing of the Constitution the slaves were considered merely as chattels. But the argument is quite overdone, for can we imagine any constitution allowing men to be elected to represent chattels? Happily, the Constitution never referred to the slaves as chattels. Ironically enough, the Dred Scott decision did not provoke a fraction of the resistance that the more constitutional decision of May 17, 1954, has provoked.

6

ASSOCIATION

From the scroll of the ancient prophet Amos there comes a proverb that has never lost its truth and freshness. Remonstrating with his people for their rebelliousness against God, the prophet asks, "Can two walk together, except they be agreed?" (Amos 3:3). The question is full of dynamite not only for an ancient nation, but also for the whole modern world. Let those peoples representing the extremes of pigmentation consider this question. Can white and black walk together except they be agreed? I single out these extremes for the reason that if black and white can learn the song of harmony, then all those who come in between can sing it also. But if they cannot become masters of this harmony, then neither can they sing themselves, nor can those in between. True, there may be those who will sing when no true harmony exists, but such is the singing of calloused hearts, not the spontaneous music of joy, honesty, and freedom.

True harmony among men depends on agreement. Where there is no agreement, there can be no harmony. Where there is little agreement, there is little harmony. Where there is broad agreement, there is great harmony. Two soloists make a duel, not a duet. The duet is most harmonious when each partner seeks to blend his talent with the other to the utmost of his ability. Behind their harmony stands the spirit of agreement. But what about those who obstinately refuse to agree? They must be endured until God breaks their pride, for vengeance belongs not to men but to God alone.

But there can be no genuine agreement unless there is genuine understanding. Two individuals cannot be called friends if they are not acquainted with each other. And the degree of the friendship is determined by the depth of the acquaintance. If the acquaintance is shallow, the friendship will be shallow. If the acquaintance goes deep, then it is possible for the friendship to go deep and to develop into a profound mutual understanding. What one desires the other desires; what one abhors the other abhors; what one feels the other feels. Such empathy cannot be achieved when one party is ignorant of the desires and aspirations of the other party. Nor can it be achieved when one party gratuitously claims to understand fully the other party and to know just what he is striving for. Too often we hear naive whites say they know what the Negro wants. They say he wants "social equality" and that his final objective is "interracial marriage." These misinformed persons betray a morbid preoccupation with sex. So fearful are they of their sexual prerogatives that their sense of justice is completely eclipsed. Witness the Emmet Till case where murder on the Lord's day was justified, and that for a minor offense. When this is the "understanding" that whites have of blacks, there is little wonder that there exists no harmony between them in certain areas.

While harmony depends on agreement, and agreement on understanding, in human relations the most basic ingredient of good understanding is *association*. Without association there can be neither understanding, nor agreement, nor harmony among men. Of course the ethical problem of sin underlies all strife among men, and no true harmony can be established among creatures who strive against God. Yet

Christians who profess to have found peace with God have been woefully slow in realizing the implications of that peace in their relations with their fellow-men. The Christian who stands against association has necessarily a shallow view of God. When we pray "Thy will be done on earth as it is in heaven," and do not cease to strive to establish *our* will on earth, our prayer can hardly be called sincere. Many people say the races will all be equal in heaven, but not on earth, therefore let us not try to be equal on earth. But such people cannot sincerely pray the above prayer; nor would they be happy in a heaven in which their freedom to disparage is curtailed. The love of God does not dwell in the hearts of those who withhold their "love" from the handiwork of God. I fear they shall not see God, for how can they love a God who has made so many people they dislike?

We must dismiss as extremely naive the attitude of those who associate after a fashion with one or two Negroes and who feel that they are thereby well informed on all racial problems and may speak as authorities. The world has heard enough from these "experts" with their easy solutions.

Segregation strikes at the very heart of good human relations, for it rules out the kind of association necessary to improve human relations. Association based on a master-servant psychology, or on a superior-inferior psychology, can never be productive of genuine harmony. We hear loud voices from certain quarters say that the races dwell peacefully in our city, county, or state. But the stubborn truth is that such boasted peace is only outward and is indeed a very shaky peace. Within there is distrust and fear, ready to erupt at the slightest provocation. All attempts to justify the systems of segregation or apartheid as according to nature and therefore right, violate all the rules of psychology, ethics, and reason. Remove all the shaky props that have been erected to uphold segregation, and the system will crash heavily to the ground with all its hollow framework ringing loudly round it. Association on a segregated basis does not produce or nurture good human relations.

While the walls of segregation enforced by law do not of course exist everywhere, even where they do not exist, the observing eye can easily detect a pattern of segregation. I speak now of mental segregation. There are many who decry the awful system of segregation that prevails in the South today. They decry the external signs evident everywhere reminding the races of their pigmentation or lack of it. Yet they themselves have isolated their minds behind a mental wall of segregation, sometimes more impregnable than the external walls of segregation in the South. They engage in limited association from behind this wall, but it never occurs to them that their brand of segregation is also obnoxious. They can never succeed in bringing about harmonious relations among men for the simple reason that they do not try. They see the splinter in their brother's eye but not the log in their own. They are as opposed to genuine association as are the legal segregationists. Their opposition to segregation springs not so much from the rejection of all segregation in principle as from the rejection of the one means of attaining a common end. And to these we must say that their efforts cannot succeed in bringing about harmony among men. They may succeed by default, *in spite of* themselves, but not *because* of themselves. Good human relations are impossible where free and voluntary association is denied by legal enactments, but just as difficult when discountenanced and punished by social ostracism.

We have spoken of two types of segregationists: the mental segregationists and the legal segregationists. Though the latter expands his error to the limit, the former is equally unable to set the proper pace for good relations among men. What must these give up in order to be more serviceable to their own social needs and the social needs of all men? What is the psychological block that prevents them from that association that alone will provide a proper basis for understanding, agreement, and harmony? In my estimation it is a false concept of "race" itself. When a people or "race" separates itself from other segments of mankind and makes extravagant claims as to its greatness and purity, it not only puts asunder what God has put together, but also sets out on the road to racial tyranny, a road that leads ultimately to destruction. The "race" concept is a divisive concept. It erects false barriers and inspires false hopes. I do not deny that there are marked characteristics among different peoples, since wherever there is relatively close interbreeding, there will develop marked characteristics. Take representatives of the five so-called races in the world today. Separate them on an island and let them replenish the island for a few hundred years, and they will develop marked characteristics and will no doubt look different from all their original ancestors. And just as this new "race" would be creating a desperate error if it claimed "racial superiority" over its neighbor races, so all races who make such claims are in desperate error. Racism of any kind, whether black, white, or anything in between is destructive of good human relations and should be repudiated by all thinking people. He who would be at a loss without the feelings of race solidarity needs to reconsider the basis of his hope. If his hope is in racial solidarity, it is a vain hope as it does not have the support of God. If his hope is in God, he does not need the prop of racial solidarity to bolster him, for he who has God has all, and he who has not God has nothing.

With the rejection of racism in all its forms there should be put in its place a balanced emphasis on the unity of the whole human race. I say "balanced emphasis" lest our minds be led to the opposite extreme of a naive unity that does not seek to understand the differences among men. The recognition of the unity of the whole human race is not in itself the cure for the social ills that plague mankind. Differences must be studied and understood. But the basis of such understanding rests on the truth of the unity of the whole human race. Previous mention has been made of the doctrine of evolution, the acceptance of which in the writer's view stands as one of the chief bulwarks against good human relations. Surely it is significant that the doctrine of evolution has never contributed to bettering social relations among "races." On the contrary it has erected horizontal, physical, social, and psychological barriers between men. Inspired by this doctrine Caucasians have spread themselves over the face of the world, making injustice to other "races" the rule rather than the exception. Evolution professes to establish organic unity not only between all men, but between man and beast. But in the practical outworking, evolution not only establishes permanent differences between so-called inferior and superior races, but it also brings out the beast in man in its justification of the treatment that the "superior races" have accorded "inferior races." It is without doubt that evolution has served as the handmaid of racial solidarity. It has served to strengthen racial solidarity, a concept we have seen to be adverse to genuine harmony among men. Evolutionistic racism overemphasizes *similarity* in the animal and plant kingdoms, and overemphasizes *dissimilarity* in the human sphere. The result of the former is the rejection of the biblical view of creation. The result of the latter is the rejection of the biblical view of the unity of the human race.

Having seen that harmony among people distinguished by accident of color or features cannot be achieved without association, it remains to discover just what is involved in such association. Mere association without a goal would be meaningless. But what should the goal be? It will conduce to a clearer understanding of the question if we first eliminate what the goal should *not* be.

The goal should not be racial dominance. The whole emphasis of the writer is to expose the false foundations and the inevitable collapse of racial tyranny.

The goal should not be amalgamation. To strive simply for amalgamation shows a lack of depth in one's ideals. Simple amalgamation is only external. Good human relations spring from within. Amalgamation might conceivably be a by-product of good human relations, but as an end in itself it is an unworthy ideal. Yet amalgamation must not be looked upon as a thing that must never come to pass, for the same blood flows in the veins of all peoples. All races have sprung from Adam and are therefore organically related.

The goal should not be integration if by integration *is meant the working together of "races" whose racial ideas are left undisturbed*. These "races" would then be working together in spite of their racial ideas, a relationship that can hardly be called harmonious. Since the Supreme Court decision of May 17, 1954, the word *integration* has grown up to be quite a monster, shaking the very foundations of this great republic. We can express only praise for this great decision so worldwide in its implications, so true to the letter and spirit of the Constitution. And I share the hopes and aspirations of all who desire a more perfect bond of union between the diverse peoples of this nation, and of the world. The success of "integration," however, depends upon the rejection of all forms of racism. The destruction of segregation must be preceded by the destruction of the ideas upon which segregation is based. Integration can succeed only as the minds of men are set free from the narrow bounds that a racist ideology requires. To replace a white racist ideology with a black racist ideology is not the road to good human relations. What we need is not another race ideology, but freedom from all racism.

The evils of racism are abundantly clear to even the most casual observer. If one pleads ignorance of the practical out-working of segregation in America or apartheid in South Africa, he can hardly be unaware of the evils of Nazism, which was the quintessence of race ideology. The world vigorously repudiated the racism of Nazi Germany. But until racism itself in all its forms is repudiated, the world may have worse than Hitler to contend with. Integration must not therefore settle down into the stifling atmosphere of a racial stalemate of "you follow your racial aspirations and I'll follow mine." The offspring of such an attitude is racial competition, and racial competition fosters an attitude of racial elimination. Unless integration, therefore, transcends the narrow limits of race it is doomed to failure.

We have seen what the goal of association should *not* be, but the question still remains, "What should be the goal of our striving?" We can best answer by differentiating between the ultimate and the immediate goal. The ultimate goal should be the glory of God. All that falls short of this glorious end is worthless as far as our relationship to God is concerned. All the works and strivings of men should be in praise of God for His wonderful goodness to the children of men. And even this would not begin to exhaust the debt of love and praise we owe Him. Should men bring about the most perfect society the world has known, and yet fail to do it in praise and honor of the Almighty God, by Whom, through Whom and to Whom are all things, all their efforts would be futile as far as their relationship to Him is concerned.

Our immediate goal should be good human relations. I emphasize *human* relations as over against "*race* relations." "Race relations" leaves racial ideas intact. The concept of human relations rises above the restrictions that a psychology of "race relations" necessarily imposes. It opens the door of the mind to a higher relationship—one fruitful of genuine harmony. Such a view involves a number of concepts and attitudes, basic among which are:

1. The recognition of the image of God in all human beings.
2. The realization that all men are neighbors in the biblical sense of that term.
3. The love of one's neighbor as one's self.
4. The rejection of all forms of racism.
5. A stress on similarities rather than differences.
6. A readiness to praise the accomplishments of others.
7. A willingness to accept one's own limitations.

Perhaps many reading this chapter will ask themselves, "Will it work? Can you get people to cooperate in the manner described in this chapter?" But the prime question is not "Will it work?" but "Is it right?" We put the cart before the horse when we begin with the pragmatic philosophy of "whatever works is good." A great deal of injustice can parade under this banner. We must first settle the question "What is truth?" and only after this question is settled may we address ourselves to the question "What is duty?" When the true way is discovered, then we are obligated to walk in it. The pragmatic philosophy directs one to *act* first according to what he considers expedient, and if he succeeds, to declare his act right.

But truth is not so discovered. Truth that is stable must be anchored to a stable standard. The Bible is such a standard, as the Bible alone reveals the true God, as well as the will of God for all men. Our procedure should therefore be to find the true view of human relations and to follow it faithfully. To reject the truth because "it won't work" is to show a disposition of heart that is not inclined to receive the truth.

Before leaving the discussion of association there is yet another problem that must not be overlooked. I refer to the view espoused by people like Booker T. Washington. Without doubt Booker T. Washington was a great man by all standards. Rising from the depths of slavery he succeeded in establishing Tuskegee Institute, which still stands today as a monument to his greatness. From the position of a despised slave, he rose to win the respect and admiration of kings, queens, presidents, and statesmen. His humility and sincerity shine forth in his autobiography, *Up from Slavery*, in which he relates with pathos and dignity the struggles, fears, and hopes that characterized his earthly sojourn. The following is not meant to lessen his greatness but to throw light upon a profound problem with which he grappled.

September 18, 1895, was perhaps the greatest day in the life of Booker T. Washington. On that date he delivered an address at the opening of the Atlanta Cotton States and International Exposition at Atlanta, Georgia. He speaks of this occasion as "one of the incidents in my life which seems to have excited the greatest amount of interest, and which perhaps went further than anything else in giving me a reputation that in a sense might be called national" (*Up from Slavery*, p. 206). He says his chief desire was "to say something that would cement the friendship of the races and bring about heart cooperation between them" (p. 217). In his stirring brief address he announced a philosophy that, although politically sound and strategically expedient, could hardly be expected to cement actual friendship between the two races. Speaking of social equality he said, "In all things that are purely social we can be as separate as the fingers, yet one as the hand in all things essential to mutual progress" (pp. 221–222). We shall return to discuss this declaration after a brief resume of the reception accorded the address.

An editor of the Atlanta *Constitution* had this to say: "I do not exaggerate when I say that Professor Booker T. Washington's address yesterday was one of the most notable speeches, both as to character and to the warmth of its reception, ever delivered to a Southern audience. The address was a revelation. The whole speech is a platform upon which blacks and whites can stand with full justice to each other." The *Boston Transcript* commented editorially, "The speech of Booker T. Washington at the Atlanta Exposition, this week, seems to have dwarfed all the other proceedings and the Exposition itself. The sensation that it has caused in the press has never been equalled." James Creelman of the *New York World* telegraphed his account of the meeting to that newspaper. I quote part of it as follows:

> Mrs. Thompson had hardly taken her seat when all eyes were turned on a tall tawny Negro sitting in the front row of the platform. It was Professor Booker T. Washington . . . , who must rank from this time forth as the foremost man of his race in America. Gilmore's Band played the "Star-Spangled Banner" and the audience cheered. The tune changed to "Dixie" and the audience roared with shrill "hi-yis." Again the music changed, this time to "Yankee Doodle," and the clamor lessened.
>
> All this time the eyes of the thousands present looked straight at the Negro orator. A strange thing was to happen.

A black man was to speak for his people, with none to interrupt him. As Professor Washington strode to the edge of the stage, the low descending sun shot fiery rays through the windows into his face. A great shout greeted him. He turned his head to avoid the blinding light, and moved about the platform for relief. Then he turned his wonderful countenance to the sun without a blink of the eyelids, and began to talk. . . .

His voice rang out clear and true, and he paused impressively as he made each point. Within ten minutes the multitude was in an uproar of enthusiasm—handkerchiefs were waved, canes were flourished, hats were tossed in the air. The fairest women of Georgia stood up and cheered. It was as if the orator had bewitched them.

And when he held his dusky hand high above his head with the fingers stretched wide apart, and said to the white people of the South on behalf of his race, "In all things that are purely social we can be as separate as the fingers, yet one as the hand in all things essential to mutual progress," the great wave of sound dashed itself against the walls, and the whole audience was on its feet in a delirium of applause. . . .

The roar might swell ever so high, but the expression of his earnest face never changed.

A ragged, ebony giant, squatted on the floor in one of the aisles, watched the orator with burning eyes and tremulous face until the supreme burst of applause came, and then the tears ran down his face. Most of the Negroes in the audience were crying, perhaps without knowing just why.

At the close of the speech Governor Bullock rushed across the stage and seized the orator's hand. Another shout greeted this demonstration, and for a few minutes the two men stood facing each other, hand in hand.

After the enthusiasm had died down, and people began to give more serious attention to the Atlanta address, Washington admitted that many Negroes came to feel that he had not been true to them, yet he stuck to his guns and won many to his side. But the complaint is justified. Social separateness is the language of the Brahmans, the segregationists, the evolutionists, and the apostles of apartheid. Social separateness is a denial of good human relations. The fact that Washington did not personally follow a policy of social separateness lends weight to the supposition that his declaration was a political move designed to give the Negro a breathing spell.

Washington's optimism was boundless, yet the present situation in the arena of "race relations" indicates that such optimism was in need of a liberal dose of pessimism. Commenting on the political future of the Negro he said, "My own belief is . . . that the time will come when the Negro in the South will be accorded all the political rights which his ability, character, and material possessions entitle him to. I think, though, that the opportunity to freely exercise such political rights will not come in any large degree through outside or artificial forcing, but will be accorded to the Negro by the Southern white people themselves, and that they will protect him in the exercise of those rights." In this prediction Washington was far off the mark. The only political rights that Negroes enjoy have come only through agitation and pressure, and in many areas political rights are still denied even the most subservient "Uncle Toms." Since the ruling of the Supreme Court in the case of *Plessy vs. Ferguson* in 1896 permitting "separate but equal" facilities for Negro citizens in interstate transportation, the South has been free to provide "separate but equal" education to its Negro citizens, but it never has. Negroes therefore began to press for entrance into the state-supported schools of their native states so as to obtain the best education available, but this was denied them. Court rulings in favor of Negroes desiring entrance into state-supported schools gave impetus to a movement in many states to provide equal but separate facilities for Negroes. But the desire for the right to a decent education is now too great, and separate education is rightly suspected as a means of perpetuating second-class citizenship.

By no means am I pessimistic over the race situation. On the contrary, the ideological developments in the field of sociology and human relations are cause for optimism. The Uncle Tom mentality, one of the greatest roadblocks to good human relations, has been admirably exposed and vigorously repudiated by J. C. Furnas in his *Goodbye to Uncle Tom*. A rethinking of the whole vast subject of modern race relations, which our generation is witnessing, is certain to be fruitful of good results. There is much for us to rejoice in, and there is every indication that the principles that underlie the Constitution will become living principles for black men as well as white in every field of American life. And as the full expression of these principles has been thwarted by racist ideas, so contemporary racism must be laid in the grave in order that a genuine harmony among men may develop unmolested. Such harmony can come only as genuine association is made a fact in American society.

At this point many will be confronted with a psychological block. The question of the direction and extent of association becomes a crucial one. They ask what will be the outcome of association? Will it lead to "racial intermarriage"? Their questions ring with the assurance that "racial intermarriage" is certainly an evil that must be kept at bay. As this is the last stronghold of the apostles of segregation, apartheid, and evolution, we must examine the concept that is popularly known as "interracial marriage."

7

HUMAN MARRIAGE

THE CONCEPT OF racial superiority and the opposition to "interracial marriage" are inseparably linked. It is impossible to divorce one from the other. In my search to find an intelligible reason behind the opposition to the marriage of human beings whom God has pleased to make a little different from each other, I have been forced to the conclusion that an acceptance, conscious or otherwise, of the concept of racial superiority lies at the root of such opposition. The divine mandate to replenish the earth was given to the whole of mankind, and, when men seek to regulate this command, we can be certain they will regulate it for their own purposes and not God's. In the absence of divine distinctions based on race, by what authority do men make distinctions based on race? In seeking to examine the popular arguments against what is popularly known as interracial marriage, I have come to believe that the feeling of race superiority is the most basic element in such opposition.

My conclusions have not made me a blind advocate of interracial marriage as such. What I do advocate is the freedom of a man to live happily before God with the bride of his choice, and a woman to so live with the husband of her choice, irrespective of their color. I do not believe that one line of evidence can be cited from the Bible to show that a person of a particular "race" may only marry another person of the same particular "race."

Though many deny that they believe their race to be superior in the eyes of God, their opposition to "interracial marriage" makes their claim suspect. For behind opposition to racial intermarriage is the concept of racial solidarity. And behind the concept of racial solidarity is the concept of race preservation. Since men seek to preserve what they consider superior rather than what they deem inferior, race preservation is based upon the notion of race superiority.

As the family is the basic unit of society, to exclude the marriage relationship between those of different "races" on non-Christian grounds strikes at the very vitals of good human relations between these races. Attitudes fostering opposition to interracial marriage, which would more accurately merely be termed *human marriage*, has this effect.

While there are many who sincerely believe that they do not labor under any feeling of racial superiority, they nonetheless become quite warm and zealous in their opposition to the marriage of persons of different races. To say that there is no reason behind such opposition is in effect to admit prejudice. To admit that there is a reason is to make progress toward the discovery of the reason. As indicated above, I must conclude that the cause of this reaction is a feeling, conscious or unconscious, of racial superiority on the part of those who oppose such marriage relations.

From this it does not follow that the Christian has a divine right to marry whomsoever he pleases, for the Christian has a God-given right to marry only in the Lord, i.e., to marry another Christian. When this fact is properly understood it will not be seen as a troublesome restriction, but as a wonderful freedom. Naturally it follows that there should be no prejudice against the Christian marrying a converted Jew.

What is popularly understood by the term "interracial marriage" is commonly considered an evil that should be avoided at all costs, but in reality it is nothing more than human marriage. The institution of marriage is wrongly used when it is manipulated by men in such a fashion as to make it serve the racial aspirations of men. The opponents of interracial marriage, whether they realize it or not, are guilty of using a God-ordained institution to attain ends that are contrary to God's plan for his creatures. Racial tyranny is not God's plan for the world, and no such tyranny can long endure. Of all people, Christians should not only be free from such aspirations, but should speak out to show their utter futility.

Many racists feel that social equality means that their children are apt to marry someone of another race. This is not the case. They *may* so marry, but certainly not necessarily or even probably. Without a doubt there are, and will always be, many who will prefer to marry within their own "race," regardless of the presence or absence of social taboos or legal restrictions. Thus the continuity of both white and black races seems assured. We must guard, however, against the notion that the right of choice, and the freedom either to exercise or not to exercise that choice, belongs exclusively to whites. Blacks have an equal right of choice, and who can tell whether or not they will consistently choose black rather than white if they have the legal and social freedom to choose? The right of selection as well as rejection is involved in social equality. It is a right that belongs to both whites and blacks. To assume that all blacks want to marry whites is obviously unrealistic. It further involves the worst kind of self-flattery. Yet when choices are made of white for black, or vice versa, or anything between, and legitimately consummated, by what right may society or the state deny happiness to those who find happiness in each other.

It is not the right of one individual to decide whom another individual may marry. While parents should assist their children and do all in their power to train them to make a wise choice of a life partner, they violate their duty to God and to their children when they seek to perpetuate racial prejudice by teaching their children not to marry outside their own "race." The same observations are pertinent regarding teachers and ministers and their responsibilities toward those to whom they serve. Actually the choice of a marriage partner is a problem primarily for those who are unmarried. It is merely an academic question for those who are not free to entertain thoughts of such a relationship. Basically no individual has the right to decide whom another individual may or may not marry.

Marriage is primarily a union of souls, and it is a wonderful truth that souls do not have color. Of basic consideration for those contemplating marriage are religion, culture, and common interests in general. A good many marriage plans have been cancelled, and a good many happy marriages have been broken up, because the fleeting characteristic of skin color has been used to prevent such unions. We have already seen that the Bible erects no racial distinctions between the peoples of the earth. Those therefore who insist on such divisions will find no comfort whatsoever in the Bible.

We will now briefly evaluate some of the popular arguments used in defense of the prevailing attitude against what is popularly labelled "interracial marriage."

It is said that it is not natural. But the fact that there are millions of people in this country alone whose family tree includes ancestors of both white and Negro "blood" is ample proof that such unions are not unnatural. Moreover, it cannot be contended in the light of all the evidence to the contrary that the children of such marriages are physically or mentally inferior. In other words the normal laws of heredity and environment remain in effect. Although many states still do have laws against such marriages, they have been and are occasioned by different motives, especially those of race preservation. In effect such laws direct the divinely ordained institution of marriage into man-made channels. They overlook the revealed fact that when God commanded men to replenish the earth, He did not divide men into racial camps and tell them to replenish the earth with their own race. He gave men dominion over the animals, but not over each other.

It is said that the children of such unions will suffer. Such children are said to be rejected by both whites and blacks. But this has not been the case historically. Such children have not been and are not exposed to any more suffering than Negroes, which fact destroys the force of the argument. Indeed the argument does not bear against such marriages, but against an obstinate society that imposes its aberrations upon helpless victims. If every individual who uses this argument would, on the contrary, say, "I will not cause such children to suffer," the number would be so great as to amount to a solution of the problem.

It is said that it will destroy the preponderance of the white race. But as such preponderance does not have the promise of divine blessing, it is to be destroyed. It is vain to trust in race solidarity.

Some say they have no objection to it themselves, but since other people object, they must respect their feelings and opinion. Thus they lay the blame on society. It is difficult to see in this attitude anything more than a shifting of individual responsibility to the many.

Strangely enough, many hold that it is a sin and thus is against the will of God. These like to feel that their views are based on Scripture, and they therefore appeal to certain passages. In Acts 17:26 Paul says that God has determined the bounds of the habitation of nations on earth. But nowhere does he speak of marriage of people of different races. Yet many believe that this passage teaches against "interracial marriage." If it be insisted that Paul is speaking about marriage, the only conclusion could be that the apostle forbids marriages of peoples of different nations, for he speaks of nations, not races. This would mean that persons of different nationalities should not marry: certainly a wild conclusion. This passage is indeed a strong refutation of all racism, for Paul declares the great Christian truth that God "hath made of *one* all nations of men for to dwell on all the face of the earth." With one blow he strikes down the pagan racism of Greeks and Romans and declares the wonderful doctrine of one human race created by God.

The implications of this truth are of utmost consequence in the area of social relations. The pagan Graeco-Roman world looked upon itself as the special creation of God; others had a less favorable origin. To them Paul said that God created all men. Rome claimed the earth for herself, allowing others to exist by her mercy. But Paul declares that God has made all men *for to dwell on all the face of the earth*, indicating that others had a divine right to the earth. And now frequently do we hear the pagan expression today that this is a "white man's world." The Christian declares that this is God's world, and we live here by His divine appointment and mercy.

The ignorant still appeal to the Canaanites as if from their destiny something may be proved regarding the sinfulness of "interracial marriage." But the theory of the Canaanite origin of the Negro has been so thoroughly disproved that those who persist in that error are worthy of the denunciation implied in the words, "But if any man be ignorant, let him be ignorant." The Jews of the Middle Ages looked upon the Slavs as Canaanites; and today the Israelis denounce the Samaritans as Canaanites. The ban that God placed on Hebrews marrying Canaanites was strictly religious and had nothing whatsoever to do with race. Whenever Canaanites became proselytes to the true religion they were welcomed by marriage into the Jewish nation. A marvelous example of this is seen in Rahab the Canaanite harlot, who found grace in God's sight and in the eyes of the spies, and became by marriage to Salmon one of the ancestors of our God and Savior Jesus Christ.

Many feel that there is support for their views in the judgment of God upon the builders of the Tower of Babel. They seem to think that God established at that time racial divisions among men, to cross which is tantamount to sin. In a previous chapter we have demonstrated that nowhere are there established racial divisions between peoples in the Bible. Rather there is the most free crossing over of national lines as well as lines that may be described as racial. But what was involved in the confounding of the tower builders?

According to Genesis 11 the whole earth was of one language. As they journeyed eastward they found a plain in the land of Shinar and dwelt there. They got the idea of building a tower "whose top may reach unto heaven." They said "Let us make us a name, lest we be scattered abroad upon the face of the whole earth." Their whole attitude was anti-God. They wanted God's heaven within their reach for their access and at their choosing. They perhaps wanted a place of refuge in case God should send another flood on the earth. An ark was perhaps disdained as not sufficient for their aims. They wanted to command both heaven and earth, and lay their terms before God for His acceptance. They went about defiantly to make a name for themselves, forgetting the name of God their Creator. And God came down and frustrated their ambitions and confounded their language. It is to this divine judgment that linguistic differences among nations owe their origin. There is not the slightest hint in the whole account of racial separations; certainly marriage is nowhere involved. This passage, like the Acts passage, is grossly misrepresented when modern prejudices are read into it. Linguistic differences are not a permanent bar against marriage. And if speaking the same language removes the bar that some imagine was set up at Babel, then there should be no obstacle at all to "interracial marriage" in the United States. However, in that case there should be no marriages of peoples of different nations in Europe or elsewhere. The folly of such a suggestion, however, is obvious.

Equally obvious is the folly of appealing to the judgment at Babel to support opposition to "interracial marriage." Untold harm is done to the cause of truth when the prejudices of narrow and bigoted minds are read into the Scriptures. Sober Christians should have a higher regard for that precious Word revealed from heaven. All attempts to ground racial attitudes toward marriage upon the Bible must prove futile. The Bible deals a fatal blow to all forms of racism, whether expressed in institutions of segregation or in attitudes regarding marriage.

According to the Bible, marriage is honorable and the bed undefiled. The racist would amend the Word of God to say marriages of blacks and whites are dishonorable, even though the bed is undefiled. And if men will declare dishonorable what God has declared honorable, they will also in time declare honorable what God has declared dishonorable. And can society claim innocence when, by its very attitude of discouraging open and legitimate relations between the races, it encourages secret and illegitimate relations?

There is a passage of Scripture that oddly enough has escaped the notice both of the apostles of racial separateness and the apostles of racial unity. In Song of Solomon 1:5 we read, "I am black and comely" (Septuagint, see pg. 58). These are the words of the Shulamite, Solomon's choice love. In Song of Solomon 5:10–11 the Shulamite speaks of Solomon, her beloved, saying "My beloved is white and ruddy, the chiefest among ten thousand. His head is as the most fine gold, his locks are bushy and black as a raven." Perhaps the racist will be inclined to remove this wonderful little book from the canon of Scripture, but truth is not so easily disposed of. It should be pointed out that the word translated "white" in verse 10 would be more accurate if translated to mean a bright red, lustrous, healthy complexion. It is the healthfulness of the complexion that is in view rather than skin color as such.

As mention has already been made of the marriages of Joseph, Moses, Rahab, and Solomon, it is not necessary to deal with them again. A host of similar marriage relationships may be discovered by the Bible student. These all stand as a wonderful and indubitable confirmation of the great biblical truth that human marriage has the sanction of God. That Christians should marry Christians only is a sound biblical doctrine, but nowhere in the Bible are people urged to marry only those of the same color. Pagan philosophy must be called in to support such a notion. But let the Christian beware of pagan philosophy, for pagan philosophy carries with it pagan ethics.

The opponent of "racial intermarriage" is dedicated to the protection of something. Is he dedicated to the protection of purity of blood? But the only pure blood is that which is common to all races of men. Is he dedicated to protecting the purity of morals? He is going in the wrong direction. Purity of morals is strengthened when persons of different races who fall in love are free to marry and live happily together without being exposed to legal penalties or social taboos. Is his aim the protection of the purity of religion? True religion stands on its own, without the weak props of racism. Is his aim the protection of the color white? No one is seeking to destroy it. Is his aim the protection of the purity of the race? But there is no pure race, as all men have descended from Adam and Eve, our first parents. Is he out to protect the dominant position of the white race? His reliance on human means is futile. And since he cannot rely on God to uphold a system that strikes at the heart of Christian ethics, he faces a great dilemma. Let the racist not seek to perpetuate racial tyranny through manipulating a divine institution for his own ends. For until a white has the perfect freedom to marry or not to marry a black; and until a black has the perfect freedom to marry or not to marry a white; we cannot rightly speak of good human relations.

Many have been the narrow-minded bigots who have claimed that the infusion of Negro blood into nations has had the ultimate consequence of bringing about the ultimate downfall of such nations. A greater falsehood has never been fabricated. That very belief can bring about the dreaded consequence, and a nation may fall victim of a psychological illness of its own making. We have already seen that the ancient Egyptian civilization was black and woolly-haired, and, if they could be brought back to the world today, they would be classified as Negro. Indeed the roots of Western civilization are traceable to the great ancient Egyptians. Prejudice of any kind is self-destructive. It destroys those who sustain and nourish it, like the dog that conceals a thousand fleas under his hair, fleas sapping his strength and riding him slowly to the grave. Let others affirm the above lie; we reject it severely and eternally.

The views of human marriage espoused in this chapter may cause many to discredit the entire book. Be that as it may, to be properly evaluated the final chapter must be considered in the light of the biblical exegesis advanced in the earlier chapters and the conclusions implicit in these principles. Those who are unable or refuse to accept the concepts advanced in earlier chapters may distort and misinterpret the final chapter. But when the earlier chapters are taken seriously by the thinking Christian, he will come to the conclusion that I am seeking the Christian answer to this question. In any event, my aim throughout has been to bring forth the genuine teaching of Christianity on a subject of great moment.

We are not as close to God as we think when our religion becomes warm toward those of our own color, and progressively cool as the color difference increases. We need the birth of a new freedom from the binding snares of a narrow racism. The scales of racism must be removed from our eyes so we can see all men as the truly marvelous handiwork of God.

A backward glance across the horizon of history will present convincing proof that the glory and might of man are at best only temporary. Great nations have arisen and fallen, and their places have been taken by other great nations, which in the course of time have also mingled with the dust, never to rise again. This process is going on before our very eyes as new nations struggle to find a place in the sun, and old nations dream of past glories. But a great truth that should by now be evident to all nations, seems to be pressed farther into the background. It is the great truth that God controls the destinies of nations, and all nations that do not glory in God are made to feel the great power of God's wrath when He causes their glory to fade.

The words of the psalmist were not written in vain when he said,

> As for man, his days are as grass: as a flower of the field, so
> he flourisheth.

> For the wind passeth over it, and it is gone; and the place thereof shall know it no more.
> But the mercy of the Lord is from everlasting to everlasting upon them that fear him, and his righteousness unto children's children;
> to such as keep his covenant, and to those that remember his commandments to do them. (Ps. 103:15–18)

The prophet Isaiah announced the same truth when he said,

> All flesh is grass, and all the goodliness thereof is as the flower of the field:
> the grass withereth, the flower fadeth; because the spirit of the Lord bloweth upon it: surely the people is grass.
> The grass withereth, the flower fadeth; but the word of our God shall stand forever. (Isa. 40:6–8)

Let the peoples of all nations be wise and take heed to the word of God, the truth of which is so clearly demonstrated in history.

In this book I have sought to show the folly of all who glory in the flesh rather than in God. And as all racism is a form of glorying in the flesh, I have sought to turn the thoughts of my readers to the contemplation of the glorious fact that differences among men only reveal the greater glory of God and are meant to contribute to cooperative unity rather than competitive divisions, to sweet harmony rather than bitter strife, to wonderful love rather than suicidal hate. For heaven and earth will rejoice together when the sons of men have learned the wonderful truth that in God's sight no flesh shall glory.

Appendix

THE CHURCH AND SOCIAL CHANGE

The constancy of change is the most predictable attribute of any society. Even resistance to change is part of the ever-changing scene of human existence. One of the greatest obstacles to man's peace of mind is the assumption that one's world will be the same through the endless ages. Many have lost touch with reality by denying the existence of what is, or affirming the existence of what is not.

So overwhelmed was Heraclitus with the inevitability of change that he concluded that *all* reality is in a constant state of change, and that the only thing that does not change is change itself. Heraclitus' view, when limited to created reality, is a profound contribution to the history of thought. For not only does all matter undergo a process of change, but so do social structures as well. Without doing violence to the biblical doctrine of creation, one might say that all created reality is ever changing. Only He who made the heavens and the earth, the Alpha and Omega, the Great I AM, is ever the same, and through his changed people he ever renews the face of his creation.

We have already implied that the church is part of the ever-changing social orders and that she, too, undergoes change. As the tool of God, the church is the *instrument* of change, calling men from the worship of the false gods of wealth and fame, race and clan, into the glorious and wonderfully satisfying fellowship of his Son. As the tool of man, the church becomes the *object* of change and is made to conform to the patterns of those who use the church for human goals. Lest I be misunderstood at the outset, however, let me make haste to say that the church as the body of Christ is indestructible and the gates of hell shall not prevail against it. Its life is divine in origin, and He who gives life to the grass and the butterfly certainly will not deny life to those whose hope for eternal life is in his Son Jesus Christ.

The problem to which we will address ourselves is, what is the role of the church in social change? The church may institute change or resist change; it may be carried along by it, or it may strengthen the good elements of change; it may seek self-preservation by an act of withdrawal from society, or it may lose its unique identity by conforming to social patterns which defy basic biblical concepts. Whatever choice she makes, one fact is certain—there is no real refuge from society, not even in lonely withdrawal, for there is no happiness there. Indeed we find refuge in God, but he rebuilds us and sends us back into society to do his will. Even this became too much for Elijah, so the Lord took him away from it all in a fiery chariot. Our present situation may be seen more clearly if we give prior consideration to the past involvements of the church in social change.

PAST PERSPECTIVES

The impact of the apostolic church on society may best be seen on the background of the type of society into which it came. We are accustomed to speaking of pre-Christian culture as Graeco-Roman. The content of Graeco-Roman culture was developed by the Greeks, while the Romans were more successful in the application of Greek culture, militarily and administratively. It is our purpose to examine briefly a part of the social content of Greek culture, for which there is no better source than Aristotle, one of the profoundest thinkers of all time.

Aristotle's Ideal Society

In his *Politics* Aristotle has given us not only his own view of the ideal society, but also a reflection of the world-and-life view shared by his countrymen. According to Aristotle, some people are slaves by nature, and it is proper and just to war against men intended by nature to be slaves but who will not submit. Slavery is not a tolerable evil but a positive good, an integral part of wealth-making. Labor was disdained as a task for slaves only. Aristotle says further, "That in a well-ordered state the citizens should have leisure and not have to provide for their daily wants is generally acknowledged, but there is a difficulty in seeing how this leisure is to be attained" (1269a). And again, "Certainly the good man and the statesman and the good citizen ought not to learn the crafts of inferiors except for their own occasional use; if they habitually practice them, there will cease to be a distinction between master and slave" (1277b). Again, "No man can practice virtue who is living the life of a mechanic or laborer" (1278a). Speaking of the best form of government he says, ". . . the citizens must not lead the life of mechanics or tradesmen, for such a life is ignoble, and inimical to virtue. Neither must they be husbandmen, since leisure is necessary both for the development of virtue and the performance of duties" (1328b).

The social and ethical implications of the above views are indeed far reaching. They encompass a disdain for labor to the extent of not providing for one's own daily needs, the glorification of a leisure based on the blood, sweat, and tears of persons considered to be inferior. It was thought that in such a society absolute justice is within the grasp of those only who avoid common labor. It becomes just to subjugate forcefully inferiors and to expose weak infants to die. There is no social relationship in either class that escapes the distortions imposed by such a view of life.

The logic of such a view when personalized would run as follows: I, Aristides, am of noble birth and must have leisure in order to achieve virtue. That fellow, Epictetus, was born to be a slave; consequently I shall make him my slave to take care of my daily wants so I can have leisure. It is just for me to enslave him by force. It is unjust for him to resist, for his resistance is contrary to nature. He has no rights but the right to submit. He is not a citizen, nor indeed can be. He is forsaken by God, for if God loved him, he would have made him like me. Neither dignity, nor family ties, nor any of the normal human emotions can be recognized in him, for he and all like him are born slaves and shall be so unto the thousandth generation. How else can I have virtue and the favor of the gods? How else can our state have security?

Thus life for Epictetus becomes deranged and grotesque. But it is no less grotesque for Aristides who must spend his leisure seeking ways of keeping the inexplicably clever inventions of Epictetus from effecting his freedom. But the problems of a grotesque society become most acute when the oppressed group endorses the ideals of the oppressing group. Strife, war, and bloodshed become the order of the day, and such a society becomes the playground for all of the vilest passions of mankind.

Opposing World-and-Life View of the Church

The Greek social and political ideals largely permeated the Roman world. It was into such a world that the church made its entrance with a world-and-life view diametrically opposed to the prevailing opinions. Far from disdaining labor, the Son of God was himself a carpenter, a calling he bore with grace, dignity, and contentment. And those whom he called into his service were men who would have been considered slaves by birth by the sages of Athens. But Jesus and his apostles had a totally different view of labor. To them it was a calling from God which they performed in obedience to God. They did not disdain husbandry, for they had long known that the first occupation of man was husbandry. And to any who might come among them and expect not to work, Paul said, "If any would not work, neither should he eat."

What to the Greeks was leisure, the mother of virtue, became to the apostles idleness, the mother of mischief. Christianity placed upon labor a divine stamp of approval giving it a dignity it had never known before. It rightly castigated idleness as the source of trouble and disharmony in society. And though Paul never recommended slavery, he reassured the slave that his station in life did not remove him from the favor of God, but that even though a slave, he was God's free man, and the master God's slave. And thus he struck the death knell to the psychology that demands the existence of slavery as a prerequisite to virtue. In fact, it was the slave concept that became the center of the Messianic message of Isaiah, who spoke of the coming Redeemer as the Suffering Servant or Slave.

The church by being the church wrought a transformation of society that can best be described as one of the most profound social revolutions of all time, for the world in time was to see kings and nobles bow the knee to the Carpenter of Nazareth and accept with eagerness the doctrines spoken through common laborers. Neither Jesus nor the apostles were social reformers pure and simple, but their teachings had social implications which were in direct conflict with the prevailing opinions of their time. They preached the love of God for all men without regard to human attributes of any kind. They preached a love of God so profound and intense as to make a candidate for divine fellowship of the lowest of human beings. The very dregs of society who found no home on earth, found a glorious home in God.

But the basic tendency of human nature to strive for earthly supremacy based on human attributes survived the assault of apostolic Christianity and has reappeared in different forms, and it is still with us today in doctrines of national, racial, and economic superiority.

Medieval Class Distinctions

The Greek view of life made a deep impression on medieval culture. Social structures were built around the notion that people were born noble or serf, the upper class inherently superior, and all ruled by a king who ruled by divine right. Labor was disdained with contempt much like that of the Greeks. Unhappily, however, the church had come to accept the class distinctions laid down by society. The social separation between serf and noble was very nearly absolute. The serf was bound to the soil to a life of misery and poverty, the luxuries of life being reserved for those few who were born to fortune. So powerful was the grip of this idea on society that it took several hundred years to break the rule of kings in most of the nations on earth.

It took, however, a religious upheaval first of all to lay the groundwork for the political philosophies that were later to command the allegiance of men. That religious upheaval is known as the Reformation. With the Reformation came a new emphasis on the inherent value of every individual before a just God. And again labor came to be looked upon, not as a diversion from human dignity designed only for slaves, but as a calling from God which must be accepted with dignity. Once again the way was prepared for men to find true dignity through the knowledge of God. For without the true knowledge of God, man cannot find a proper estimate of himself.

Reformation and Man's Worth

Underlying the thinking of Luther was the doctrine of the intrinsic worth of every man before God. The social implications of such a doctrine involved a rejection of the class distinctions upon which medieval society was based. The peasants were ready to destroy such distinctions with more force than wisdom. With the same concept undergirding his thinking, Calvin went on to apply the newfound doctrine to all realms of life. Original Calvinism was indeed a movement for religious reforms, but no less was it a movement for political, social, and economic reforms. It was a movement involving a total world-and-life view—a new religious view of society, a new religious view of politics, a new religious view of economics. It challenged the prevailing opinions that divided men into classes of nobles and peasants, into which the nobles were born fortunate and the peasants born unfortunate.

Society was geared to the notion of the inherent inequality of these classes. But the prevailing view was only a social doctrine by which the wealthy kept their wealth. The new doctrine was a direct challenge to the old. In time, political thinkers were to arise, moving in the tradition of the inherent value of every individual, and asserting that all men are created equal. Not finding anything in the traditional world-and-life view on which such a doctrine could be based, Jefferson had to insist that the views he espoused on the equality of man were self-evident. That God gives to individuals certain inalienable rights which kings must recognize was a very novel and radical political doctrine in Jefferson's day. But the doctrine of the inherent value of every individual in God's sight, which grew out of the Reformation, was widespread enough in Jefferson's day to provide fertile ground for the growth of the political branch which became the United States of America.

Over against the contemporary view that labor was degrading, Calvinism emphasized its dignity. Over against the contemporary view of the divine right of kings, Calvinism placed the king under divine law and laid out his limitations. Over against the contemporary doctrine of the inherent inequality of men, Calvinism emphasized the inherent equality of all men before God. Thus was the church, by being the church, the instrument of social change.

Modern Slavery

But any notion that the Aristotelian social ideal was dead would be gravely erroneous. For even while the echoes of the Reformation were still reverberating in Europe and America, slavery of the worst kind took firm hold in many lands that were being transformed by the Reformation. While some of these countries went abroad and made virtual slaves of peoples they captured, America brought a large quantity of slaves to her homeland. And with the blessing of church and state millions of human beings were uprooted from their homeland and transplanted to hostile and brutal surroundings. But this time the chief objects of the slave hunters were the dark-skinned peoples of Africa.

This fact seems to point to a color consciousness that was beginning to take hold in the western world. It is difficult to pinpoint the reason for the development of white color consciousness. Perhaps the geographical exploits of European explorers showed them that the white man was a minority in the human family. Perhaps they sought self-preservation in color solidarity and Pharaonic treatment of non-whites.

However it got started, it became a dominant factor of western global politics; so much so that a new concept entered the pages of history, the concept of the "white man's world."

As a means of maintaining and extending white supremacy, racial separatism or segregation became the order of the day. Almost all social, political, economic, and religious institutions came to operate on a racially exclusive basis. In the thinking of many, white became synonymous with right, and even today in Alabama, at election time, all voters are faced with the symbol of the Democratic Party in Alabama, the slogan of which is "White supremacy for the right."

The Church's Shame

This equation of white with right is one of the most ludicrous monstrosities of history. Even Aristotle insisted on cultural integrity as a prerequisite to a genuine claim to superiority. And even that was anti-Christian. But under the doctrine of white supremacy, anybody with a minimum of melanin in his skin is superior to those with whom God was more liberal with melanin. This in itself is astonishing enough. But to realize that the church has played a major role in creating and maintaining such an absurdity in the church and in society is hard to accept as a present reality.

This very moment a minister languishes in jail in Atlanta for attempting to take Negro children to a "white church" in Atlanta. Hundreds of Negroes have been jailed for simply attempting to enter the sanctuary of "white churches." I say before God and all the angels, it is a shame that a doctrine more ungodly than that of Aristotle holds such great sway in the church today and prospective worshippers, with the words of Jesus and Paul on their lips, are hauled from church doors to jails. Jesus said, "Come unto me all ye that labor and are heavy laden, and I will give you rest." But in the name of

Jesus many "white churches" say if any Negroes come here, we will give them jail. In a very real sense, Jesus has been put in jail. But only the unenlightened pagan mind may expect Jesus to stay locked up, for no jail has yet been devised that can contain his Spirit. In such a situation one is reminded of the admonition of Calvin to King Francis I that the church can exist without visible form.

The church by word and deed must declare it human folly to trust for security in the color of a man's skin. No church, race, or nation is truly secure because of skin color. God has inscrutable ways of exposing the false confidence of all whose hope for security is in any other than in God himself alone. Egypt once boasted in its blackness of skin, but not only was the power of Egypt broken, but in time its original blackness ceased to be characteristic of the whole nation.

Before entering into a discussion of present realities, it would be profitable to consider briefly Calvin's views on civil disobedience. In the chapter on Civil Government in his *Institutes*, Calvin insisted that rulers are appointed by God, and that subjects owe obedience to all their rulers both the good and the bad. It is not for subjects to correct tyrannical abuses, but only to obey and suffer. However, if any ruler should give a command against God, such a command should be disobeyed and completely ignored. He also maintained that "equity, being natural, is the same to all mankind, and consequently all laws, on every subject, ought to have the same equity for their end."

Calvin and Civil Disobedience

Where equity is by law not the same to all men, Calvin in this chapter does not recommend tactics of civil disobedience as a means of attaining equity. Thus it might appear that Calvin would be opposed to such methods. However if we consider the circumstances of his times, and his actions as well, it was only by civil disobedience that he and his followers were able to exist. According to Calvin, he was a good, faithful, and law-abiding subject. But according to those in charge of the dominant institutions, he was a pestilent fellow and a seditious rebel, subverting all order in society.

The world-and-life view introduced by the Reformation was so much out of accord with traditional thought and institutions that the very maintenance of the new doctrines was an act of civil disobedience. And as the uncompromising proponent of the "new doctrines" as they were called, Calvin was the champion par excellence. The governing power, being in the hands of the champions of the status quo, had become so oppressive that the only way one could exist with dignity was through civil disobedience. This situation is upon us in full force again in our day.

When unjust laws require a man to dehumanize himself before he can drink water or eat a morsel, or even sit down, what is left for a person with a sense of dignity to do than to resort to civil disobedience? At the present time the law is on the side of those who insist on the dehumanization process. On that side, too, are many who claim to move in the tradition of the Reformation with its insistence on the value of the individual. But if there is anything to the doctrine of the intrinsic worth of each individual, and I believe there is, then one cannot be true to that doctrine, and at the same time practice or approve of the practice of degrading an individual for reasons of color, national origin, or religion.

Personal Reflections

One day as I sat in my car in a busy shopping center in Birmingham at noon, I became conscious of the fact that I was hungry, and my stomach began to complain. I looked out over the many stores and saw that I was surrounded with restaurants, hamburger shops, drug stores, and five and ten cent stores with lunch counters. Occasionally a playful breeze would bring gently to me a gust of air full of appetizing odors. I had money in my pocket; I was a citizen of the country; I could speak the language of the people; I was dressed and clean shaven; I had degrees from outstanding American institutions; I was a law-abiding, decent, upright, tax-paying citizen, and a Christian minister. But I was hungry.

Then I saw in one glance the ugliness of segregation. For I could not go into one of the many public places and eat a lunch with peace. I was too dumbfounded to be mad, and just hungry enough to think deeply about this unspeakable situation. I saw a great problem: a problem that I could not solve by going away from it; a problem that white people cannot solve by driving me away from it. For if all the black people were driven from Alabama, still the problem would not be solved, but only confirmed.

We have heard that it is Christian to share, and certainly this is true. Yet in parts of our country if a Negro finds himself hungry, and is surrounded by restaurants and lunch counters, he cannot so much as buy a morsel of food and eat in peace. Being a man is of no avail. Being a Christian is of no avail. Being a tax-paying citizen is of no avail. Even a Communist from Russia or any foreigner could satisfy his hunger in peace and dignity, but a tax-paying Christian and loyal citizen cannot enjoy such a privilege. The penalties for attempting to do so are insults, expulsion, and jail.

Cry for Liberty

I find it hard to understand why the white man refuses to recognize that to which he gave birth. It was he who revolted against the so-called God-ordained class distinctions of feudalism. It was he who raised the standard of liberty for the common man, for the oppressed of the earth. Now the cry of black men for liberty is but the echo of the white man's cry in the American and French Revolutions. This is the cry of a legitimate baby of the American Revolution. But the father does not wish to hear it. Rather he tries to make himself believe it is the very cry of the illegitimate child of the Russian Revolution. But the cry is from a legitimate baby, a baby which cannot now be pushed back into the womb of history, a baby determined to see life for himself. He may at times be weak and helpless, but he is here to stay. We must not forget that the American Revolution did not destroy England. It only released the energies of a great people and enabled them to try the wings of nationhood.

The bravery of the white Southerner is not brought into question by the present demands for justice. The willingness and the ability of the white Southerner to fight for what he believes in is an undisputed fact of history. But we are now one nation, faced with a greater "menace" than the desire for freedom. Shall we spend our energies in the defense of privilege, and thus negate our whole history? Shall we weaken ourselves by trying to stifle the legitimate aspirations of Americans for liberty? Shall we curse Patrick Henry for saying, "Give me liberty or give me death"? Shall we consider it a crime for black Americans to be liberty-loving Americans? Rest assured that when we become weary from fighting one another, we will have neither the mind nor the ability to face a common foe. The struggle for liberty from unjust tyranny did not end with the American Revolution. It only began.

And the present struggle for liberty is but a continuation of the spirit of the American Revolution. Destroy it, and liberty is dead.

But I am still hungry. I am still a Christian, a minister, and a law-abiding, tax-paying citizen. And yet in many parts of this country the law deprives me as a citizen from the enjoyment of the most elemental human rights. In this context Calvin's view on equity needs to be re-emphasized. Hear him again say, "Equity, being natural, is the same to all mankind; and consequently all laws, on every subject, ought to have the same equity for their end." It is significant that Calvin does not argue the point but states it as a universally accepted maxim. It would be good if we could be as broad in twentieth-century America as Calvin was in sixteenth-century Switzerland.

PRESENT REALITIES

Having attempted to view with brevity some of the past involvements of the church in social change, it now remains for us to consider present realities. It would require separate treatment to trace the development of the Negro protest movement in America. Suffice it to say that there was never a time in American history that the voice of Negro protest was not heard. Resistance to slavery sometimes took the form of violence, such as the Nat Turner Rebellion of 1831, and the John Brown raids. In time, the whole country was plunged into four years of violence. But the country was under the leadership of a poor man who made good, rose from abject poverty to an honorable and lasting place on the pages of history. But the spirit of violence overcame him, and he was assassinated.

Following the Civil War, Frederick Douglass championed with great vigor the cause of the oppressed. Booker T. Washington sought a solution through accommodation, and W. E. DuBois pressed for political freedom. But these all lacked the mass appeal that was to develop under Marcus Garvey.

Under the leadership of Marcus Garvey the Negro protest movement took on national proportions with a mass appeal unequalled before in this country. Garvey had given up hope that America would ever be just to her black citizens; consequently he looked away from America for that society in which men of color could enjoy freedom. It is not especially significant that he looked back to Africa. This was the logical choice of a homeland. But it is very significant that he and thousands of Negro citizens of the United States were ready to depart from America, the haven of rest for white Europeans, to escape the house of bondage that America had become for the Negro. The international implications of such a move were that America could no longer pose as the champion of the free world while hiding her mistreatment of her own dark citizens. In time, however, the Garvey movement fell upon evil days and it ceased to be the threat it once was.

As the star of Garveyism declined, a new protest movement appeared in religious form seeking to gain the allegiance of the Negro masses. Like its predecessor, it expected no justice from white institutions. But unlike Garveyism, it does not seek a return to Africa for salvation, but the establishment of a separate black state in this country. In this new movement, white is no longer right, but the quintessence of evil; the white man is the devil, incapable of good; and black becomes the symbol of purity, sweet innocence, and God. Nor is it strange that such a movement should arise. For if the logic of white racism is correct, the logic of black racism is equally correct. The rejection of one necessitates the rejection of the other.

Search for Identity

Deeply involved in all racist ideologies is the problem of identity. Every person who becomes truly self-conscious must grapple with the problem of identity. He must answer to his own satisfaction the question "Who am I?" The answer that a person gives to this question determines his basic attitude toward people and toward life in general. The person whose identity is first and foremost in national origin will be at a loss among persons of a different national origin. His personality will not blossom and mature as it would if he were in the group with which he has identified. His own identity sets the limits of his own personal development by limiting the ability of his personality to coalesce with "foreign" personalities. He builds a wall around himself and pretends that nature placed it there. Such an attitude becomes a nationality complex to those whose highest identity is national. The damage to the personality is the same whether one's highest identity is nationalistic or regional or racial or in color.

Fortunately there are many personalities that rise above the lesser identities that so often cause strife. What the world needs now is a large supply of personalities capable of rising above the limitations of racial and color identities. Television and the airplane have made all cultures contiguous, and the ability to reach an understanding quickly can be of strategic value.

Security in Christ

Since the search for identity is also a search for security, both the search and the answer must come under the scrutiny of the Christian world-and-life view. The highest and most meaningful identity is that in which one sees himself first and foremost as a human being, and as such, a special creation of God, of no value without him, of infinite value with him. Without God, man cannot boast, for he is nothing. With God, man cannot boast, for God is All. He whose identity is truly with God through Christ has no need of an identity or security which excludes those esteemed to be a lower grade of humanity. The very exclusion is itself evidence of the lack of true security. The exclusion proves the inadequacy of the identity.

The truly secure personality has identified with all creation and with God through Christ. Only on such a plane of life can one understand the words of the apostle, "All things are yours . . . and you are Christ's and Christ is God's." Only on this plane of life are possession and belonging compatible. He who possesses all things while at the same time is totally possessed is truly secure. But this security belongs to those who identify with the possession (creation) and the Possessor.

Deeply embedded in the Judaeo-Christian tradition is one of the most profound social concepts of all time running counter to the most penetrating discoveries of human wisdom—the idea of voluntary slavery consistent with human dignity. The Son of God became the Suffering Servant. And Paul, motivated by the supremely beautiful example of Christ, could say "though I am free . . . yet I have made myself slave unto all." "And this I do," he continues, " for the gospel's sake, that I might be partaker thereof with you" (1 Cor. 9). Here one sees an identity which extends from the most "ignoble" to the most glorious. It is only on this basis that one can become "all things to all men." The social implications of such a view are destructive of all ideologies of racial, national, cultural, religious, or color identities.

Considering the medium through which the above thoughts have been derived, it remains the greatest enigma to this writer how one can profess to be Christian and at the same time be anti-Semitic.

But let us return to the Negro protest movement which today is the most widespread movement in this country seeking to bring about social changes. Some persons seem not to know what is going on in our country, while others are fearful that Communists are the cause of the present social revolution. But let us stop and consider what life is like in America for the man of color.

"Not a Man"

When a man is told from the cradle to the grave that he is not a man; when every facet of his life is made in some way to be a reminder that he is not a man; when the state and church both combine in their testimony that he is not a man; then why is it surprising when such a person finally comes to agree with society and decides that he is not a man? There is nothing unusual about a man agreeing with majority opinion. When majority opinion is against a person in a particular society, that person is in a dying state as far as that society is concerned. When society withdraws all its benefits from a person, it brings on a kind of death that is very real. Fortunately, however, God's judgment does not always coincide with majority opinion; for if it did, then Elijah would have fought in vain; Jeremiah would have preached in vain; and Christ would have died in vain, a lonely minority.

The Negro has accepted too long what white society has been saying about him. It has killed his spirit and he can now find life tolerable only in rejecting that evaluation. He is seeking manhood on his own terms as he interprets the Bible and history. It may be that in the past the white man has looked upon the Negro as a valley of dry bones. In a sense this is true, for the white man has taken away his flesh by bolting up the door of dignified progress to him. The great question facing us today is "Can these bones live?" As long as dignity is denied to them, the answer must be "No."

No doubt the success of Elijah Muhammed in making "these bones live" is in the new sense of dignity with which he inspires them. The tragedy is that such basic documents of human dignity as the U.S. Constitution and the Declaration of Independence are not his source of inspiration. For this country has not yet accepted the Negro into full enjoyment of liberty and dignity and it does not yet appear that it ever will. Still more tragic is the fact that the Negro's tax money becomes a source of strength for those who deny them liberty.

In contrast to the American and French Revolutions which broke away from the prevailing opinions, the current Negro revolution is seeking to break into the prevailing opinions of equality and exact justice for all. It is possible that he may fail, but he will not again be the valley of dry bones he once was. His emerging concept of history provides one outlet. His willingness to go to jail without fear provides another outlet. Some day he may take Jefferson seriously and get violent. It would still be within the tradition of the American Revolution.

From Passivity to Action

The day of passive acceptance of the status-quo is gone. Militant groups of all varieties are active all over the country seeking to bring about a more just order, seeking to exercise the ballot in some areas without fear of death or economic strangulation, seeking to satisfy the needs of nature without having to go to jail in the attempt, seeking to change the patterns of schooling in which the dry bones are made, seeking to worship at churches which say their doors are open to all, but who throw in jail Negro citizens who seek peacefully to enter. What makes it all so inscrutable is that one must be a good, loyal, tax-paying citizen of the United States before he is eligible for these unspeakable indignities. Even a foreign enemy, if he is white, can take for granted the privileges which loyal Negro citizens have to go to jail for. This is a present reality.

Much is being said about the preservation of states' rights and responsible government. But much of this talk is no more than a dignified front for anti-Negro sentiment. There was a time when no such front was needed, but now some who are basically anti-Negro have left it to the Nazis, the National States' Rights Party and the Klan to wallow in public philippics against the Negro, while they publicly profess friendship for the Negro and at the same time, under the guise of fighting for states' rights and constitutional government, they fight against every effort to make life more tolerable for *the* Negro. They would do well to bear in mind that no government has the right to deny a man his manhood.

Peaceful Protest

Violations of citizens' rights by public officials are beyond calculation and apparently without remedy. One of the most basic rights of our democracy is the right of peaceful protest. Yet when Negro citizens seek to protest peacefully the inequities imposed upon them, local and state authorities repulse them with vicious dogs, fire hoses, billysticks, and cattle prods while federal observers observe. In the last few years thousands of peaceful protesters have been hauled to the jails of our land, until it is becoming proverbial that the jails are for people who wish to be free. Convictions of officials for violations are almost nonexistent. Of the more than 300 complaints of rights violations which were made to the F.B.I. in Birmingham during the 1963 demonstrations, there was not even one single prosecution, not to mention a conviction.

Last fall a Negro youth who was being jeered by white youths passing by in a bus, and who was struck in the chest with a rock thrown from the bus, retaliated by cutting the arm of one of the youths that protruded from the bus window. For this horrible crime he was at first charged with willful intent to murder. The charge was later reduced and the youth was finally sentenced to six months in jail, and he is currently serving that time.

But on the same day that a house of worship was bombed in Birmingham, and the lives of four lovely girls were snuffed out, a white youth, returning from a meeting of the anti-Negro, anti-Semitic National States' Rights Party, shot and killed a Negro youth riding on a bicycle. For this relatively harmless diversion, he was given seven months, and even that sentence was suspended and a judge put him on two years' probation, which would be altered if it interfered with his schooling. It is almost as if he were rewarded for his marksmanship. This says many things to the Negro.

Another Negro lad, fleeing for his very life from Birmingham policemen, was shot through the lung and killed on the spot. The lad had every right to flee, knowing what to expect from lawless policemen. But he slipped and fell and was shot dead. When a youth is shot fleeing across the Berlin wall to freedom, it makes the front page in Birmingham as a barbaric atrocity. But when a Negro child, innocent, unarmed, and fleeing for his life, is shot in the back and killed, the act is justified by local officials. This says many things to the Negro.

Danger of Extremism

Bombings and dynamitings, shootings and killings followed in the wake of the Birmingham Demonstrations last year. Birmingham demonstrated for freedom, using the pre-American Revolutionary methods of peaceful protest. But it seems that America did not appreciate non-violent peaceful protest. It is hoped that a realization by the white man that the Negro is not by nature non-violent will restrain him from seeking to thwart completely the method of peaceful non-violent resistance so ably championed by Martin Luther King. The destruction of this method will not bring domestic tranquility to our borders but will prepare the way for an approach more in keeping with the American Revolution. Already the spirit of Nat Turner is showing signs of revival. And in world politics today such a spirit might find allies all over the world, whereas Nat Turner was very much alone.

The turmoil in which we find ourselves in this country is ample evidence of the fact that we are in the midst of a profound revolution. Our Constitution is being put to its most severe test since the Civil War. It is my firm conviction that the Constitution will survive, no thanks to those who use the Constitution to justify the dehumanization of man. It is also my firm conviction that the church should throw its moral weight against the racial injustices that still characterize American society. The church must give men a hope in God that can stand without the crutches of racial, national or color identity. It must undermine every ideology which encourages men to seek security in outward appearances, for all these will certainly fail. Only the true and living God never fails.

Facts of Social Revolution

A realist approach to the problems facing us requires the recognition of certain facts. First, there is a social revolution going on in the United States today of very great magnitude. It cannot be wished away. This revolution is an outgrowth of the improved economic and educational status of the Negro.

Second, this revolution is motivated, not by foreign ideologies, but by the American ideology of individual freedom and equal justice for all. The Negro has heard the slogans of freedom, liberty, and justice in America for the last 300 years. It should not be surprising that he is taking it more seriously than ever before. That he has hope in America in spite of the past is all to the good. To repress that hope is subversive of the basic framework of our government. One of the most unpatriotic things one can do is to seek to smother the light of liberty in the name of patriotism, or Americanism, or constitutional governmentalism.

Third, the goal of this social revolution is not amalgamation, for amalgamation is a fact everywhere; nor is the goal black domination, for not only is that unrealistic but it is untenable historically and logically; nor is it preferential treatment, though this is understandable; but the goal is human dignity.

Fourth, the method is currently non-violent peaceful protest. I say currently because it is not certain that this method will remain the predominant method. One of the most vulnerable positions in the current social revolution is the position of leadership. Leadership can change so rapidly that one has said that the militant leader of today is an Uncle Tom tomorrow. It seems that one type of leadership provokes a more militant type of leadership, which in turn provokes an even more militant type of leadership. Where it all will end is not altogether certain. But it will end when the goal of human dignity has been achieved.

It is true that our country's image suffers when scenes of violence are televised around the world. This is regretted very much, for we suffer when our country suffers. But we do not see why we should bear all the suffering while our country enjoys a false image around the world of being the haven of the oppressed. Why should we pay taxes to support the government when we are by force kept from the enjoyment of elementary rights and then be silent while the government presents itself to the world as the champion of liberty? I am not suggesting that we, like Thoreau, refuse to pay taxes to a government considered to be unjust, but it would be a very powerful demonstration if practiced on a large scale. It would be more dignified than a filibuster.

Our Country and the World

Our democracy stands now in the full light of world opinion; we desire the friendship and respect of all freedom-loving peoples. We stand at the crossroads of the twentieth century.

Over against our system of individual freedom stands a system which denies individual liberty and champions the rights of the state. Both systems, however, stress freedom. But the "freedom" of Communism is a state-provided freedom maintained at the expense of individual liberty and forced upon the people by a government the people did not freely choose. On the other hand, our freedom is not created and maintained by the government at the expense of individual liberty. Rather, through the exercise of individual liberty, the government itself exists. Its task is not to create and bestow rights but to protect the God-given rights of men.

Both systems are engaged in a struggle to gain the allegiance of men. For peoples who have been oppressed by autocratic governments, the appeal of individual liberty exemplified in our Constitution is irresistible. Free and alert people will always choose individual liberty rather than slavery to the state. Which road will the emerging nations take in the next few decades? Their choice will determine the kind of world they will face in the next century. And their choice will also help to determine what kind of nation we will be in the next century. What we do about democracy at home will help in large measure to determine the choice the emerging nations will make. Unless we can demonstrate that freedom and individual liberty are a reality for all citizens in our democracy, the whole cause of freedom will suffer, and the forces of totalitarianism will be strengthened. Our failure will contribute to the failure of freedom in other parts of the world. Their failure can in turn accelerate our own demise.

Christian Duty

It is always the duty of God's people to be a light to the world. There are no considerations that can relieve us of this responsibility. Too often one hears from the white minister such sentiments as, "I know what ought to be done, but if I try to do anything I'll get put out of my church and they will get an extremist." This approach does not relieve the minister of his obligation to do what he knows he ought to do.

Nor is the honor of the church upheld by silence in the face of injustice, nor is the true church preserved by failure to do what it knows to be right. The church in Germany did not save itself by its silence in the face of Hitler's budding inhumanities, but it might have saved Germany if it had preached without fear the biblical concepts of justice and righteousness in the church and in the state. We cannot preserve the church. That is God's responsibility. Our task is to do what God requires of us—to do justice, love mercy, and walk humbly with God.

C. Herbert Oliver was born in Birmingham, Alabama, in 1925. A graduate of Wheaton College and Westminster Theological Seminary, he wrote and published *No Flesh Shall Glory* while pastoring Bethel Orthodox Presbyterian Church of Ludlow-Smyrna and Houlton in Maine. He returned to Birmingham in 1959 and, starting the following year, served as the executive secretary of the Inter-Citizens Committee, interviewing victims of police violence and filing reports at a state and federal level. By the mid-1960s, the situation in Birmingham had improved. Oliver moved to Brooklyn, New York, and fought for equality in the schools as chairman of the governing board of the Ocean Hill-Brownville school district until 1970. He was the pastor of Westminster Bethany Presbyterian Church in Brooklyn for twenty-five years, retiring in 1992, and continued his activist work after his retirement as he protested the mass killings taking place in Sudan during the Darfur Conflict in the early 2000s.

ALSO FROM P&R PUBLISHING

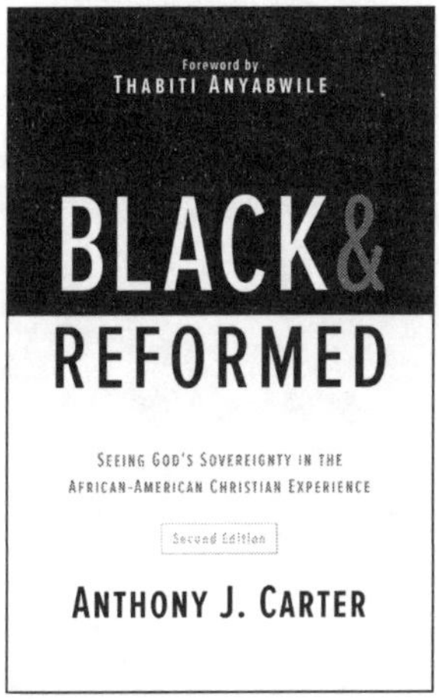

Carter shows how Reformed theology best speaks to African-American experience—and demonstrates how Black experiences and traditions can and should deeply enrich our theology, no matter our heritage.

"As an African American I am delighted with the publication of this book. It will serve as an excellent introduction to Reformed theology for the emerging Black Reformed community in the United States. I anticipate that it will be a great resource for church planters and anyone else seeking to reach the Black community."

—Anthony B. Bradley

"When I met Anthony Carter several years ago, I detected a rigorous mind, a righteous concern for racial justice, and a Reformed vision of God—a rare combination. Since then I have wanted to be a listener. Now this book makes that easier. May the Lord of nations use it to shape a powerful movement of God-centered Christians from all peoples who have tasted suffering."

—John Piper

ALSO FROM P&R PUBLISHING

Black, Hispanic, and Asian scholars and leaders share advice on building relationships with minority communities and valuing the perspectives and leadership of minority Christians—not just their token presence. They seek to help evangelicalism more faithfully show the world that the gospel brings together people from all tribes, languages, and cultures.

"This is a terrific book . . . a game changer. . . . If you are tired of the usual arguments about race, as I am, this book will wake you up with some new ideas."

—**John M. Frame**

"Anthony Bradley pulls together some of the church's best minds to confront the problem of 21st-century evangelicalism with grace and truth. Those willing to look honestly at the facts . . . may yet lead our cherished institutions to true repentance."

—**Eric C. Redmond**

ALSO FROM P&R PUBLISHING

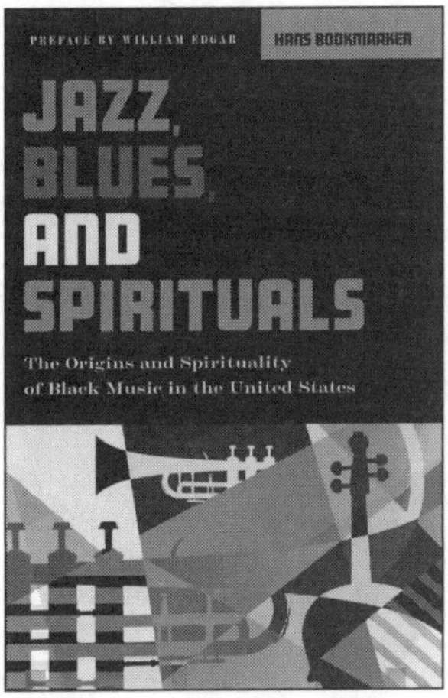

Rookmaaker's classic music history explores the development of Black music in the United States from its earliest days until the 1950s—describing the origins, rationale, and interplay of diverse new genres and providing insight into the music's spiritual background and qualitative differences. This new edition features a preface by William Edgar, an accomplished jazz pianist and a professor at Westminster Seminary.

"A robust and diverse contribution to the world of music comes out of the Black experience in America. . . . Hans Rookmaaker gives us this American story through the lens of God's work among a people. We are brought into the beauty that springs out of joy and sorrow intimately tied to a hope rooted in God."

—**Irwyn L. Ince**

ALSO FROM P&R PUBLISHING

Scripture says that human beings are God's image bearers and worthy of our time and respect. From that truth, we can draw important guidelines that will transform our conversations, relationships, and lives together. Pastor Tim Shorey blends the marvelous with the mundane, laying out a COMMUNICATE lifestyle built on eleven practical decisions we need to make when we converse.

"Requiring truth-telling and vulnerability, while recognizing the full humanity of others, and embracing both our uniqueness as well as our unity in Jesus Christ as an image of the gospel, *Respect the Image* is a focused and helpful plea for greater listening and learning in all our relationships."

—**Ruth Naomi Floyd**

Did you find this book helpful?
Consider leaving a review online.
We appreciate your feedback!

Or write to P&R at editorial@prpbooks.com
with your comments. We'd love to hear from you.